THE DEFIANCE

A Socio-Economic Problem Solving
(Edited Book)

MOHAMED BUHEJI
& DUNYA AHMED

authorHOUSE®

AuthorHouse™ UK
1663 Liberty Drive
Bloomington, IN 47403 USA
www.authorhouse.co.uk
Phone: 0800 047 8203 (Domestic TFN)
*   +44 1908 723714 (International)*

© 2019 Mohamed Buheji & Dunya Ahmed. All rights reserved.

No part of this book may be reproduced, stored in a retrieval system, or transmitted by any means without the written permission of the author.

Published by AuthorHouse 05/23/2019

ISBN: 978-1-7283-8869-4 (sc)
ISBN: 978-1-7283-8870-0 (e)

Print information available on the last page.

Any people depicted in stock imagery provided by Getty Images are models, and such images are being used for illustrative purposes only.
Certain stock imagery © Getty Images.

This book is printed on acid-free paper.

Because of the dynamic nature of the Internet, any web addresses or links contained in this book may have changed since publication and may no longer be valid. The views expressed in this work are solely those of the author and do not necessarily reflect the views of the publisher, and the publisher hereby disclaims any responsibility for them.

CONTENTS

Definitions vii
Keywords ix
Abbreviations xi
Introduction xiii

Part 1. What is Socio-Economic Problem Solving? 1
Chapter 1   Understanding Problem Solving in
            Inspiration Labs 3
Chapter 2   Shaping the Anatomy of Socio-
            Economic Community Problems
            towards Effective Solutions 27
Chapter 3   Application of Differential Diagnose in
            Inspiration Economy Labs 42
Chapter 4   Understanding the Economics of
            Problem-Solving "A Longitudinal
            Review of the Economic Influence of
            Inspiration Labs- Three Years Journey
            on Socio-Economic Solutions 52

Part 2. Defiant Case Studies 73
Chapter 5   Influencing without Power" Currency
            in Inspiration Labs: A Case Study of
            Hospital Emergency Beds 75
Chapter 6   Influence of Visualised Reflection on
            "Solving Socio-Economic Problems"- A
            Case from Youth Economy Forums 97

Chapter 7	Understanding Mechanisms of Resilience Economy- Live Application on a Complex Business Model	124
Chapter 8	Youth Unemployment Mitigation Labs "An Empathetic Approach for Complex Socio-Economic Problem"	145

Conclusion 183
Main References 185
Brief About Editors 187

DEFINITIONS

o **Problem**= A gap in the ability to find inspiring opportunities. It is a gap between where we want to be, in relevance to current situation. The problem is considered a problem when we do not know how to cross that gap.
o **Socio-Economic** = Is the science of the interaction of social and economic factors that address how social processes shape economic activity. It helps to measure the outcome of community progress attempts, because of the economic conditions or activities influencing it.
o **Socio-Economic Problem Solving**= Finding opportunities inside the socio-economic problems and overcoming challenges that lead to creating an inspiring outcome.
o **Inspiration Currency**= A means to deliver and measure inspiration that occurs through socio-economic problems solving significance.
o **Inspiration Engineering**= Finding and mapping opportunities inside a socio-economic problem, to overcome challenges and discover more possibilities for outcome and legacy.
o **Inspiration Economy**= outcomes of socio-economic problem solution that change the specific setting, or the community status and show them their intrinsic opportunities and hidden powers.

KEYWORDS

1) Complex Problem Solving
2) Socio-Economic Problems Solving
3) Breakthrough Solutions
4) Communities Problems
5) Economics of Problem-Solving
6) Vector Analysis towards Problem Solving
7) Influencing without Power
8) Innovative Problem Solving
9) Inspiration Labs Problems Solving
10) Mindset and Problem Solving
11) Socio-Economy
12) Economy of Problem Solving
13) Sustainable Development Goals
14) Visualisation and Problem Solving

ABBREVIATIONS

Active Labour Market Policy (ALMP)
Community Problems (CPs)
Differential Diagnosis (DD)
Influencing without Power' (IWP)
Inspiration Economy (IE)
International Labour Organization (ILO)
International Monetary Fund (IMF)
Lifelong Learning (LLL)
Non-Profit Organisation (NPO)
Not in Education, Employment and Training (NEET)
Quality of Life (QoL)
Resilience Economy (RE)
Small and Medium Enterprises (SME's)
Sustainable Development Goal (SDG)
Vocational Education and Training (VET)
World Economic Forum (WEF)

INTRODUCTION

This edited book comes to address a gap in literature till date about socio-economic problems solving needs, requirements, challenges and techniques which are all very important for any community's realised development. During the last few years, a collection of peer-reviewed papers were published to address such important growing discipline. The idea behind this work is to explore how the defiant socio-economic problems can be tackled, using different approaches and from different perspectives. Therefore, we target in this book to show how socio-economic problem solving works theoretically and then show a sample of case studies that illustrate the application of the approaches in different areas and fields.

One of the few references we could find nearest to this book is the work of Chang, D'Zurilla and Sanna (2004) which focused on social problem-solving. We agree with Chang et al. team that without solving community-based problems the quality of life and the well-being would be a danger. However, in this book, we emphasise that a multi-discipline approach with a focus on the socio-economic problems would create a significant contribution to the essence of life itself. In reality, this work is only an extended effort to discover the practical solutions for problems encountered in everyday living. In this work the editors target to set practical pathways that can help the readers to learn to solve community problems effectively and positively, thereby leading to generalised and durable behaviour changes.

Professor Szirmai's (2015) is one of the leading researchers credited for addressing socio-economic development issues and integrating it with the modern development economics literature. Szirmai focused on development economics and its relation to a wide range of social sciences. The work of Szirmai focused on tackling the problem of why the poor countries stay poor and how are wealth and poverty related to changes in health, life expectancy, education, population growth and politics. However, Szirmai explored the dynamics of socio-economic development in developing countries without proposing solution techniques.

In relevance to all the literature before, the **first part** of this book calls for understanding the essence of socio-economic problems solving, via four chapters, the **first chapter** targets to leave the reader with more understanding about problem solving in inspiration labs, as the problem solving have always been related to creativity, breakthroughs, development, disruption, innovation, learning, knowledge, agility, resilience and most of all inspiration. The chapters in this part of the book show the relation between inspiration economy and the process of socio-economic problem solving, including the depth in the meaning and the essence of each problem and the complexities behind it. This part includes how the socio-economic problem brings insights, persistence, perseverance and most of all better visualisation over time.

The **second chapter** is about how the socio-economic community problems are getting complicated every day, despite many developments regarding social innovation, behavioural economy and inspiration economy programs. The chapter focus on the socio-economic outcome using a qualitative approach. The anatomy of randomly selected socio-economic community problems is explored here to explain the framework that leads to an effective solution.

Chapter three explores the importance of advanced problem-solving techniques with a focus on the application of Differential Diagnosis (DD). DD is a technique adopted and developed as part of the inspiration economy project. The diagnosis used in DD helps to effectively dissect the complex problems in unstable economy or communities. With DD we can manage the extract hidden opportunities in turbulent challenging problems in a unique, yet disruptive way.

Chapter four explores the different types of socio-economic problems confronted in the three years' journey of inspiration labs carried out as part of the Inspiration Economy Project and in different countries around the world. The discussion is done for each of the economic vectors extracted for each problem. This is followed by a proposed framework on the 'economic solutions vectors' which shows how to tackle any socio-economic problem-solving using this technique. The chapter concludes with the type of socio-economic development that supports the flourishment of the targeted communities.

In the **second part** of this book takes us through different case studies of socio-economic problem solving which apply methods discussed in the previous part. The first chapter of this part, **chapter five** presents one of the main techniques of socio-economic problems solving that is believing in the capacity of 'Influencing without Power' (IWP). IWP is considered to be one of the sources of the currency of inspiration. The chapter applies IWP on a complex case of a country shortage of 'hospitals emergency beds' and how this can be solved in inspiration driven economy techniques. The authors do a comparative reference to what the literature on IWP focus compared to the problem context. In this problem, the sources and currencies of inspiration are utilised to develop the availability of regional hospital emergency patients' beds. The hospital was selected to experiment with the concept of IWP, i.e. to solve the problem without the utilisation of extra power or resources. The research method consists of the analysis of the case-study specifically in its role in creating positive influence through specific hidden solution approaches.

Chapter six shows how the economics of problems solving works using reflection techniques. The influence of the socio-economic problem value is integrated with mechanisms of visualised reflection. The youth experience and mindset are evaluated while dealing with the socio-economic problems before, during and after the forums.

The seventh chapter of this book builds the bridge between resilience economy and socio-economic problem solutions. The application of complex business models, show how resilience make the models more independent and thus ease the road towards more inspiration driven economy. In this work, the author tries to link between resilience and socio-economic through answering the demands for sustainable dynamical systems when attempting community problems solutions.

The final chapter focus on solving complex problems like the issue of youth unemployment that is increasing every day due to the amount of graduating youth. The restatement of the problem is part of its solutions, where youth are found constrained from smoothly entering the labour market. Therefore, the issue of youth unemployment is not only a United Nation Sustainable Development Goal (UN-SDG), but remains to be an important complex global challenge that needs deep solutions. This chapter reviews all the past and contemporary solutions to the youth unemployment problem.

Finally, the target of this edited work is to excite the readers to tackle complex socio-economic problems from different perspectives, without hesitation or procrastination. It represents a 'spirit of defiance' as the name chosen for this worked. The world still, and more ever today, needs more collaborative efforts and sharing of innovative problem-solving techniques, especially those that would raise the dignity of human beings and ensure a common realised development.

PART ONE

WHAT IS SOCIO-ECONOMIC PROBLEM SOLVING?

CHAPTER 1

Understanding Problem Solving in Inspiration Labs[1]

Introduction

The world is full today of new challenges and unprecedented problems. These problems vary from being political, to being economical, to being social, to being technological, to being environmental and then legal.

Too scientific, technical, complicated and specialised problem solving proven to have limitations compared to evolving world needs and demands. Literature in need for a redefinition of the anatomy of problem-solving and see how to create innovation and inspiration in its process (Hippel, 1994). The process of problem-solving need to be investigated from the way it handles the constraints and challenges and how these can be turned into possible sources for discovering opportunities.

Lately, more research has focused on tackling socio-economic problems from different perspective and ideas (Sawery, 1990; Qin et. al., 1995; Buheji and Thomas, 2016; Hut, 2017), reported on

---

[1] Buheji, M (2017) Understanding Problem Solving in Inspiration Labs, **American Journal of Industrial and Business Management**, 7, pp. 771-784,

behalf of the World Economic Forum that the world couldn't solve many issues as poverty, rising unemployment or income inequality, weak financial systems, gender inequality, low long term planning and investments besides last but not least the rise of non-communicable diseases (NCDs) to the prohibitive costs of care, particularly in developing countries.

There is still a gap also in the literature from the point of understanding the cognitive processes and psychological interactions that happen during the operation of problem-solving which is affected by the problem statement (Davidson and Sternberg, 2003; Jonassen, 2000; Bransford et al., 1986).

In this chapter, the researcher would open the type of literature review that needs to further investigated and focus on studying the role of problem statement as one of the ways that enhance our readiness to deal with the problem anatomy, process and structure in the most suitable and possibly cognitive and psychological contribution.

Literature Review

Anatomy of Problem Solving

What is a problem? It is a situation that want to be changed, or an opportunity want to be discovered. A well-defined problem is easy when it comes to pure science like math, physics, or even chess. i.e. you can get clear solutions, procedures and logic would play a significant role in defining its outcome. The rule for the solution usually is clear, but still, you have to work for it!

However, in reality life is full of ill-defined problems where the rules are not clear, and usually there is one "correct" solution, but there are best alternatives. Learning to solve problems is usually limited to class rooms and in formal educational settings until today.

This is because mainly of not understanding the anatomy of problem-solving and what it needs more. Solving a problem has never been based on instructions or discussions only, all the realised problems that were solved and helped humanity towards real development came from working on the field with trial and error.

Each problem has its constructs and codes that differentiate it from other problems. Thus each problem has its structure, specificity and complexity. Thus each problem engages a different cognitive process that needs different data collection and synthesis approach.

Thus, mental activities for each problem should differ in its approach when it goes through the process of acquiring, retaining and using the knowledge and it might extend even to the level when synthesis, inferences and conclusions are withdrawn.

At the time of acquiring information and knowledge about a particular problem that might go through mental image representations of either objects or events. Whether these objects or event are present or not physically present. This gradually builds visualisation about the problem anatomy, but with some probability for errors (Hippel, 1994).

The Psychology of Problem Solving

The competitiveness of any problem solver or problem-solving methodology has always been dependent on psychology (Davidson and Sternberg, 2003). Problem-solving is about thinking which in turn depends on the type and extent of the behaviour directed toward attaining the solution that usually not readily available, in real life problems (Gick, and Holyoak, 1980; Kendler, et al., 1962; Jonassen, 1997). The psychology in problem-solving says that the problem must be understood correctly to accurately solve it, as it is the most important cognitive activity in any daily or professional process (Jonassen, 2000).

D'Zurilla et al. (1971) see that people mostly deal cognitively with a problem the same way, as our mindsets root problems, i.e. when an external event happens, people choose to see only one side of the story, and then interpret the solution around it. D'Zurilla and his team saw that people need behavioural modification as through this modification people can create a mindset that would be able to accept a variety of alternative solutions. Much earlier, Norman Peale (1898-1993) have witnessed this earlier when he saw that how people think about a problem is more important than the problem itself, as to how problems are stated and presented affects problem-solving a great deal.

Recent studies show that inspiration physiologically is usually evoked by a problem that needs to be solved, or as a result of observing recent trends during travelling (Buheji and Thomas, 2016). The problem is also then affected by the type of thinking (Bransford et al., 1986). For example, if our mindset is controlled by convergent thinking where our attitude would be focused on finding a particular answer to a problem, the solution would be different from that of divergent thinking where our mindest generate as many possible solutions to a problem as possible. Even the solution to a problem would if the attitude of the problem solvers tends to go for incubation thinking period where they leave the problem for a time, allowing the minds to unconsciously to find the best solution or to find from it an insight.

More research has actually shown that there are different approaches to problems solving and way of implementing innovative solutions (Terwiesch and Xu, 2008; Leonard-Barton, 1995). Found that introverts and extroverts differ even in the way brain is stimulated and how it is processed. For extroverts, their ability to take well detailed observation make their ability to tackle the problem and availability of solutions faster, however not necessarily better solutions. Therefore, the introverts, might be more value added in dealing with problems that need careful monitoring and long term planning.

Importance of Inspiring the Problem Solving Process.

The European Commission report (2011), emphasises the need for new economic resources that address the rising demands of human welfare needs, be it health care, education, resource efficiency and environmental challenges. Through inspiration, humans are self-motivated and even more equipped to solve social, economic, political, technological and environmental problems.

The problem-solving process as shown in Figure (1) starts with defining the issue of the problem and therefore generating ideas from that scope. Evaluate the problem situation and see the possible ideas, then redefine the problem and make a selective decision.

Figure (1) Problem Solving Process

Define Issue(s) of the problem & Generate Ideas

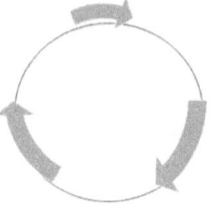

Define the Problem then make the Selective Decision

Evaluate the situation and possible Ideas

In order to inspire the model of the problem-solving process, handling the mental blocks that face ideas and opportunity generation is needed. The mental blocks are a collection of attitudes that prevent us from thinking something different. The problem is not that there are problems, as Theodore Rubin quoted, but rather that the problem is that human is expecting otherwise and thinking that having problems is a problem. Thus to inspire a way of thinking and to handle the problems before thinking about solving them (Bransford et al., 1986).

The Handbook of Inspiration Economy shows how the inspiration to the problem-solving the need to shift from the school of the few experts to the general public to face the complex problems of unemployment, or to alleviated level of poverty; due to reaching sustainable limits (Buheji and Thomas, 2016). This means there is a need to shift the mindset from the school of scarcity thinking to abundance thinking. Therefore, one could conclude that inspiration plays a role in stretching our limits as human beings thus lead to more creative solutions in solving uprising life problems.

Stages of Inspiration of the Problem Solver

D'Zurilla et al. (1971) seen that the stages of problem-solving starts with general orientation with problem and definition for its formulation, then the need to generate alternative solutions to that specific problem before creating a proper decision making.

However, in Buheji and Thomas (2016) it was debated that it could not really formulate the problem characteristics sometime or even generalise it before it takes it through trial and error where people would be able to try a variety of solutions and eliminating those that do not work without fear.

During inspiration Lab after visualising the problem researchers start dividing it into constructs and work our way backwards. The purpose of this whole process is not to solve the problem, but rather to use it build from it an insight, or find the blind spots that it could not see clearly. This moves our mind from the stage of observation to stage absorption where a human would be ready to realise the solution that can create real development. Therefore, one could see that insight come in literature only when the process of the problem suddenly moves from not knowing how to solve it.

Inspiration labs that were developed as part of IE total solution not only try to solve the problem permanently, but rather looks for opportunities from inside each problem and what type of socio-economic characteristics it carries. The search for the opportunity deep inside the problem, is an IC that might not be realised at first instance. Insights or development solutions might not appear till all the data are gathered, analysed and deeply interpolated.

Since the solution has to meet the development goals or create a restoration needed to restate the problem before it goes for identifying alternative solutions which should not be eliminated until they are tested. Then the solutions should be tested against the desired results.

Constraints and Challenges to Inspirational Solving Problems

In any problem-solving exercise, there would always be constraints relevant to time, cost and most important of all the mindset or the psychological preparedness when handling any problem (Davidson and Sternberg, 2003).

One of the most challenging psychological constraint that tends to face when solving any problem till date is the functional fixedness. This is a mindset issue. The type of mental set, the inability to see an object as having a function other than its usual, or what been experienced with, build solid assumptions that leads to specific solutions. Gick and Holyaok (1980) study support this relation, since they have seen that the capacity of the brain would be able to build better analogical relations which would influence the processes of problem-solving.

Constraints and challenges of the mindset define our tendencies of how problems are approached, since the habits control our perception or thought.

Mohamed Buheji & Dunya Ahmed

Problem Solving as a way for Discovering Opportunities

Our understanding of a problem depends a lot on the way it is seen and visualise opportunities. The way our mindset sees opportunities help us to discover hidden areas of thoughts and open for us unforeseen opportunities which are continually around us. Therefore, Sun Tzu clearly saw that real victory comes from finding opportunities in problems. This change in the mindset of seeing every problem as an opportunity to raise our appreciation of problems as a gift for discovery.

The continuous handling of different problems helps us to use synectics, to join two irrelevant elements of a problem or two problems to discover new opportunities. Most of the recent discoveries which come from more than one discipline and disrupt product or service pathways come from this methodology. Synectic mechanisms are fundamental for an inspiration based economy, since it helps to increase our probability to create an inspiration using our intrinsic powers. However, in order to enhancethe discovery of opportunities, which can redesign the words, meanings, and definitions or use metaphors (Jonassen, 2000; Gordon, 1961). This synectic process makes the strange familiar and the familiar strange.

This methodology is heavily used in inspiration lab out which represented in table (1). The lab works on generating lots of ideas and combining existing ideas in different ways for new purposes, seeing the same thing but thinking of something different, selecting unique and useful ideas and solutions to everyday challenges (Bransford et al., 1986).

In order to keep discovering human should avoid fixation of the mindset where the same approach would be followed. The field work and consistent piloting in the inspiration lab help to evaluate the alternative opportunities one at a time then to eliminate those that do not meet the desired criteria.

Problem Solving and Quality of Observation

One of the challenges and weak capacity for problem-solving is the dependence on third-party reporting where low reliability and the low quality of observation of data could be collected. Problem-solving capacity differs when the information needed by problem solvers is readily available (Hippel, 1994).

May this justify Einstein way of seeing things and where he was quoted saying that people should never impose their views on a problem; one should instead study it, till the solution reveal itself.

The locus of problem-solving may iterate easier when the observation was collected by unpolluted noise, i.e. the data collected with clear use of the senses from the field, or through primary data collection that uses interviews, focus group besides questionnaires and surveys. This reduces the iteration and also reduce the cost of the data collected while the availability of the information would also improve at the time needed (Hippel, 1994). It is thus creating less complexity to the problem. Therefore, Dale Carnegie used to say that the biggest problem is choosing the right thoughts, which one add that it usually comes the quality of information synthesised.

Application is a level where we ensure that the inspiration cycle is realised. Through applying activities as 'a codification' of the problem and then 'classification' before final 'stratification' to the problem, the human can make their mindset reach the status of realisation. The more observations are collected through: implementation, trial and testing, changing the setting, and using a different level of illustrations and demonstrations, the more it can enhance our chances to capture later and even create opportunities with confidence.

Part of the application that will help enhance our ability to discover the hidden spots inside any problem is our ability to absorb the essence of the problem and what messages it does send. In order to reach this level, more classification analysis is needed to use supporting with the drive to enhance our forecasting. The absorption here would come more and more through modification and exploration of the problem definition and way it is presented or constructed.

Once in-depth analysis is started, evident absorption might start the realisation stage. This stage will confidently try to arrange, connect, divide, infer, separate, classify, compare, contrast, explain, select, breakdown, correlate, discriminate the problem. This stage starts to think empathetically, where to start to see the parts and the whole.

This should help to build synergetic practices that would lead to rational processes that involve the way of thinking and handling a problem all the way until a solution. One can argue thatproblem-solving process and statements, therefore, are very important for creating better stratification (pull thinking), systematic explorations that would lead to new unforeseen concepts as shown in Figure (2).

Figure (2) Use of Problem Statements to build up steps for Concept Generation

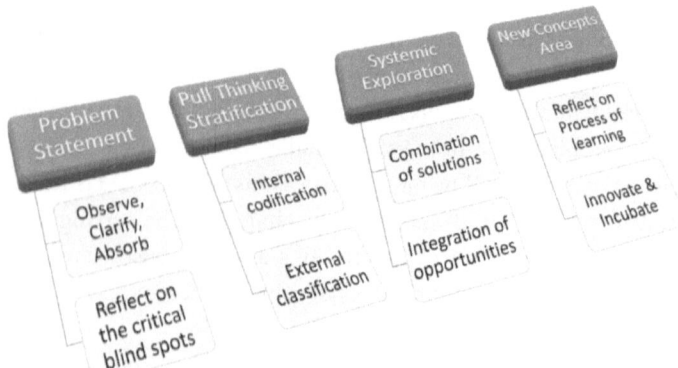

Human Cognitive Processes and Experiential Learning during Problem Solving

Takashi Yamauchi (2002) studied in detail the problem solving mental processes which occur when people work toward determining the solution to a problem. Newell and Simon (1972) mentioned two main approaches that move human cognition. The first approach is called the Gestalt approach which focuses on how people represent the problems. In this approach, the solving of any problem involves a reorganisation or representation of the problem. The other approach focus on information processing which the problem solving becomes like a search finding process.

Hippel (1994) studies show how problem-solving is costly to acquire and transfer. However, it is found to be very important for the locus of innovation thinking and competitiveness. Training through problem-solving is considered as a form of self-control and self-development program. While learning how to solve a specific problem are discovering new ways of how to deal with life and are even developing our mindset to be more lean and agile. The mindset learns new attitudes, behaviours and more effective way of how to respond to challenges.

Thrash et al. (2010) showed that as a result of the experiential learning that is built by trying to solve life challenging problems, as in the inspiration labs, the process of ideation occurs.

Distraction as a way for Problem Solving

Distraction is the highest form of inspiration, because when it is distracted more prone to think outside of the problem. Overcoming distraction or disruption can lead to an inspiration that leads to something real and tangible. Many scientists create intentional psychological interference with obstacles for students to stimulate their ability to learn beyond the traditional environment. (Davidson and Sternberg, 2003; Gick, and Holyoak, 1980; Kendler, et al., 1962).

Jack Penn said one of the secrets of life is to make stepping stones out of stumbling blocks. What prevents us from finding a solution is not a distraction, but somewhat functional fixation. Therefore, there is a need to appreciate sometimes ill-structured problems since, in reality, they have more probability for the engagement of learners.

Well-structured problems are constrained problems with convergent solutions that engage the application of a limited number of rules and principles within well-defined parameters. Ill-structured problems, even though start with fuzziness and distraction, possess multiple solutions, solution paths, fewer parameters which are less manipulable, and contain uncertainty about which concepts, rules, and principles are necessary for the solution or how they are organised and which solution is best. Jonassen (1997) concluded that solving well-structured problems would be usually based on information processing that creates new learning, while solving ill-structured problems cognition approaches that create a totally radical change and learning.

Research Methodology

The research methodology employed in this chapter is qualitative. A longitudinal review of the experience of the 53 inspiration labs problems solved in 29 different business was set in Table (1). These problems or challenges were encountered during the years 2012 till 2017, as part of different projects where inspiration labs problem-solving techniques applied (Buheji and Thomas, 2016). The table was set to help study the type and level of problem statements utilised to create the necessary solution to the socio-economic issues identified. The table is meant to enable the researcher to investigate the type of problem statement used for each challenge and whether it matters in creating an inspirational solution to real-life chronic or challenging problems.

The chapter attempts to address the research question: "What is the uniqueness of inspiration lab in identifying problem statements?" Table (1) also helps to review the scarcity of use a certain level of the problem statement, the aim to investigate how it can improve the capacity for its utilisation in the future. The analysis for the problem statement would be reflected through a detailed discussion that leads to the conclusion.

Table (1) Type of Problems Solved in different scopes in relevance to Problem Statement

Type of Business	Summary of Type of Inspiring Projects/Models	Type of Problem Statement
1) Education	1- Shifting *from Competitive Schools Focus towards Inspiring Schools* 2- *Discovering the type of inspired students* vs gifted, competitive, innovative and creative students 3- Tracking of the *inspired students after graduation.* 4- Building *Curriculums that supports students inspiration*	Main Technique: Basic Problem Statement a) Observe, Clarify and Absorb b) Reflect on the critical blind spot c) Internal codification
2) Social Development	1- Improving the Quality of Life (QoL) of the Bahraini Elderly/ Geriatric Care Homes through inspiring their intrinsic powers ability 2- Inspiring the *capacity of Productive Families Program* to be more self-independent and attractive for more family members to join as employees/ owners 3- Improving the *Quality of MicroStart Families* 4- Easing the process of home care 5- Supporting *Working from Home* Program	Main Technique: Pull Thinking Stratification a) Internal Codification in relevance to types of QoL Practices b) External Classification of potential market penetration c) Combination of Solutions

Type of Business	Summary of Type of Inspiring Projects/Models	Type of Problem Statement
	6- Revaluating the **Capability of Social Allowance** Entitlement 7- Enhancing the quality and competitiveness of the productivity *of the Retired and the Disabled*	
3) Electricity Services	Improving the **speed of electricity connections** services nine times faster.	Main Technique: Basic Problem Statement a) Reflect on the critical blind spot
4) Police	1- Enhancing the ability to *trace Drug Trafficking and early detection* 2- Enhancing the role *of Prevention of Community Complains through Society Police* 3- Minimising the *Thefts incidents in Jewellery Shops* 4- Minimising the *threat of Illegal labours* 5- Minimising *Families Disputes transfer to legal courts*	Main Technique: Pull Thinking Stratification a) Internal Codification b) External Classification c) Combination of Solutions
5) Passports	1- Raising the **speed of finishing Visa's** 2- Ensuring **speed and customer services at Arrivals**	Main Technique: Basic Problem Statement a) Reflect on the critical blind spot
6) Traffic Directorate	1- Enhancing the *appreciation of Traffic Light Violation Fines* Services 2- Improving *the accuracy of Traffic Accidents Investigation*	Main Technique: Basic Problem Statement a) Observe, Clarify and Absorb b) Reflect on the critical blind spot
7) Land Surveys	Speeding up *land Surveys Services*	Main Technique: Basic Problem Statement a) Observe, Clarify and Absorb b) Reflect on the critical blind spot

The Defiance

Type of Business	Summary of Type of Inspiring Projects/Models	Type of Problem Statement
8) Foreign Affairs	1-Ensuring the *economic role of Embassies* 2-Enhancement of *Knowledge Sharing among Ambassadors and Embassy Staff*	Main Technique: Basic Problem Statement a) Observe, Clarify and Absorb b) Reflect on the critical blind spot
9) Chamber of Commerce	**Re-Establishing *competitiveness for Unstable Businesses* through Business Model**	Main Technique: Systematic Exploration a) Combination of Solutions b) Integration of Opportunities
10) Applied Science Colleges	Inspiring students to enhance their *contribution towards innovation* index by more focused projects	Main Technique: Pull Thinking Stratification a) Internal Codification b) External Classification
11) Industry Sector	1-Speed of *throughput of Environmental friendly industrial projects* that less dependent on depleting resources. **2-Enhancement of Investment utilisation** in the Industrial area through *re-design of space utilisation*.	Main Technique: Pull Thinking Stratification a) Internal Codification b) External Classification
12) Commercial Sector	**1-Enhancement of CR registration** through inspiring the reality of *'one stop shop'*. 2- *Improving the contribution of Microstate and Small Enterprises towards more profitability* and enhancing its actual contribution to the Bahraini labour Market.	Main Technique: Basic Problem Statement a) Observe, Clarify and Absorb b) Reflect on the critical blind spot

Type of Business	Summary of Type of Inspiring Projects/Models	Type of Problem Statement
13) Training and Development	**Transformation of training** to make it more focused on knowledge management than knowledge building only in the areas of ICT and Hospitality as a model	<u>Main Technique</u>: Basic Problem Statement a) Observe, Clarify and Absorb b) Reflect on the critical blind spot
14) Pension Fund	Inspiring *investment enhancement towards Local Market* Stability	<u>Main Technique</u>: Basic Problem Statement a) Observe, Clarify and Absorb b) Reflect on the critical blind spot
15) Water Services	**Minimising water loss** by *inspiring the ability to discover* the early leakages by the process of observation	<u>Main Technique</u>: Systematic Exploration a) Combination of Solutions b) Integration of Opportunities
16) Primary Care	**1-Early detection of Non Communicable Diseases** (NCD's) (Diabetes, Blood Pressure, Cholesterol and Obesity) by inspiring 2-Enhancement of Quality through **Inspiring Families** Physicians 3-Practicing **Triage to inspire a priority system in** Health Centres 4-Early **detection of Psycho-Sematic in relevance to Anxiety** in Health Centre.	<u>Main Technique</u>: Systematic Exploration a) Combination of Solutions b) Integration of Opportunities
17) Secondary Care (Hospitals)	Inspiring the **total throughput in Accident and Emergency and admissions** in Hospitals based on Urgency of the cases	<u>Main Technique</u>: Systematic Exploration a) Combination of Solutions b) Integration of Opportunities

Type of Business	Summary of Type of Inspiring Projects/Models	Type of Problem Statement
18) Secondary Care (Hospitals)	Enhancing the *availability of the Capacity of Beds Utilisation* by inspiring towards higher *discharges on time* and based on defined protocols and follow-up services	Main Technique: Systematic Exploration a) Combination of Solutions b) Integration of Opportunities
19) Public Health	Inspiration in establishing *'Intelligent Inspection' that minimise the rate of poisonous food* calls or low hygiene fines by 90% with fewer workforce resources and trustworthiness enhancement. Thus, enhancement of the reputation of fast food services that support local tourism.	Main Technique: New Concept Area a) Reflect on Process of Learning b) Innovate and Incubate
20) Health Enrichment	Enhancement *of 'QoL' practices* and style in coordination with Health Centres	Main Technique: Basic Problem Statement a) Observe, Clarify and Absorb b) Reflect on the critical blind spot
21) Psychiatric Services	Inspiration to *Manage the anxiety* to avoid reaching the level of chronic anxiety where the individual would a patient treated with medicines and reduce suicide.	Main Technique: New Concept Area a) Reflect on Process of Learning b) Innovate and Incubate
22) Quality Assurance in Education	Ensuring that **level of the student in under-performing school** meets the minimal standard.	Main Technique: Basic Problem Statement a) Observe, Clarify and Absorb b) Reflect on the critical blind spot

Type of Business	Summary of Type of Inspiring Projects/Models	Type of Problem Statement
23) Labour Fund	*Ensuring that all funded projects had made a success sto*ry through the domino's effect of Labour Funds.	Main Technique: Basic Problem Statement a) Observe, Clarify and Absorb b) Reflect on the critical blind spot
24) Municipality Services	Building a comprehensive model for local people about the *effect of recycling* in their 'LLL' abilities and 'Qualities of Life' through inspiring (Schools, Families, Local Super Markets, NGO's) to take more proactive practices toward Social Responsibility.	Main Technique: Basic Problem Statement a) Observe, Clarify and Absorb b) Reflect on the critical blind spot
25) Research and Development	1-Establishment of *Knowledge Asset register* in organisation 2- Enhancement of University or the R and D centre to *deliver multi-disciplined projects* 3- Enhancement of *Project Closure to ensure the learning and enhancement of projects* delivery stays within the organisation 4-Study *the integration between the contracted projects* and published papers.	Main Technique: Systematic Exploration a) Combination of Solutions b) Integration of Opportunities c) Start to reflect on the process of learning
26) University	Ensuring *Lifelong Learners Students* through the inspiring way of flipped class teaching and ensuring suitable preparedness for coming life challenges.	Main Technique: Pull Thinking Stratification a) Internal Codification b) External Classification

Type of Business	Summary of Type of Inspiring Projects/Models	Type of Problem Statement
27) Labour Market	S*hifting Unemployment* through inspiring the ***stratification of Human Capital data and building models in specific industries*** as per countries sustainable socio-economy needs	Main Technique: Pull Thinking Stratification a) Internal Codification b) External Classification
28) Minimising Traffic Accidents	***Inspiring traffic accidents*** reduction efforts through: a) Enhancing the ***road are designed towards worst cases,*** not best cases b) High ***availability of road maintenance*** and active learning on the black spots.	Main Technique: Basic Problem Statement a) Observe, Clarify and Absorb b) Reflect on the critical blind spot
29) Sanitary System	Enhancing drainage system design during ***minimisation of repeated blockages in the sanitary system***	Main Technique: Basic Problem Statement a) Observe, Clarify and Absorb b) Reflect on the critical blind spot

The complexity of the type of problems tackled shows that it can tackle lots of world problems through inspiration labs. I.e. can solve healthcare, poverty, educational; unemployment, safety, environmental problems through the utilisation of the process of cognitive focus that inspiration labs use and bring in.

Analysis and Discussion

Inspiration Labs as a tool for generalising Problem Solving Statement

Inspiration Labs was introduced as a technique for complicated life problem-solving in early 2010, and the first paper was written about it as a reported success story (Jahrami and Buheji, 2012). Since then lots of books and papers have been coming along in this area to cover the development and maturity of this technique over the last few years in solving problems in a different field. Table (1) takes us through the unique way and variety of solutions generated from inspiration labs that were carried out by the researcher in different settings and different cultures. The design of the inspiration labs of the different issues mentioned in table (1) helped to overcome many chronic problems that were solved through following a specific problem statement technique. This supports the work of Jonassen and Hernandez-Serrano, 2002; Jonassen, 2000; Jonassen, 1997). In reference to Figure (2), problem statements found to create waves of IC in the business model of the organisation and the targeted society. Inspiration labs shown that it can achieve new and better results, if it responds differently taking into consideration the intentions set by the level and type of problem statement as shown in the third column of Table (1) and as realized in the second column which illustrates how the problem helped us to spot better opportunities or to create new ones.

Inspiration Labs shown in table (1) illustrates the uniqueness of problem statement in the creation of field-driven ideation. This process of ideation through problem-solving enhanced the level of results and even the level of organisation contribution to the socio-economy. The results of more than 190 projects, similar in the complexity of those presented in Table (1) and in every discipline shows the importance of inspiration labs in raising the capacity of problem-solving and in enhancing the level of knowledge integration.

The learning created by the inspiration labs problem statement has both a direct and indirect influence in creating the cycle of inspiration. The main learning of all the problem statement techniques mentioned in Figure (2) can be characterised as active, collaborative, and cooperative that leads to radical change which supports the work of Qin et al. (1995).

Why Inspiration Economy Needs Problem Solving Statements?

Inspiration spirit can be created from a problem or a challenge or an opportunity that is built during the search for solutions. Failing to equip our mindsets with different waves of any of the problem statements as in Table (1) means lose of focused thinking and curiosity which creates one of the main blockages of inspiration. A society that is poor in valuing and nurturing its citizen's intellectual curiosity will suffer from lack of inspiration generation abilities which in turn affects its socio-economy. This is why IE needs Problem Solving Statement as without it cannot maintain the minimal level of curiosity that would generate the IC Buheji and Ahmed, 2016).

Inspiration based economy needs to tackle problems in order to find opportunities for breaking the shield of the mindset. This can happen through clear problem statements. Problem statement brings in opportunities which are in unstable economy help us shift towards focusing on the discovery of the intrinsic powers within the self or the targeted community.

Conclusion

Problem-solving is a dynamic balance between problems solving and opportunities discovering. Through problem-solving, we can generate options for development. The mindset that is used to solving problems statements can have more opportunities for ideations and to identify promising ideas. Through problem-solving organisations and societies, it gets more chances of putting our ideas into action.

Inspiration can be sustained through the ability to address appropriate problems statement. The more problems are solved, capacity will be increased to create judgement and to deal with failures which later build better tolerance to ambiguity.

The purpose of this chapter was to explore how the problem-solving statement plays a role in inspiration labs and the level of opportunities discovered. Our fundamental assumption in this chapter was the relation of problem-solving to the mindset. The chapter shows however that the problem statement plays a role also in solving all the complex issues tackled in the inspiration labs. Thus the capacity of problem-solving is not only related to the mindset, but in fact to the problem statement.

Even though this chapter has limitations of finding enough previous work that goes in a similar way of thinking, the researcher believes that the techniques used in categorizing the anatomy of problems and challenges faced in real life could really help in better facing more global and complex issues such the ones reported in World Economic Forum (WEF) (2017) report.

This study sheds new light for researchers about the importance of problem-solving in creating a better economy. It also has implications for practitioners as it encourages more exploration of opportunities that would inspire both social and economic aspects inside each problem by using problem statements used in inspiration labs and at a different level of problem complexity.

References

Bransford, John; Sherwood, Robert; Vye, Nancy; Rieser, John (1986) Teaching thinking and problem-solving: Research foundations. American Psychologist, Vol 41(10), Oct, pp. 1078-1089.

Buheji, M and Ahmed, D (2016) In Search for Inspiration Economy Currency—A Literature Review. American Journal of Industrial and Business Management, 6, 1174-1184. http://www.scirp.org/journal/ajibm ISSN Online: 2164-5175

Buheji, M and Thomas, B (2016) Handbook of Inspiration Economy. Bookboon. ISBN: 978-87-403-1318-5.

Davidson, J and Sternberg, R (2003) The Psychology of Problem Solving, Cambridge University Press.

D'Zurilla, Thomas J.; Goldfried, Marvin R. (1971) Problem solving and behavior modification. Journal of Abnormal Psychology, Vol 78(1), Aug 1971, 107-126.

European Commission (2011) Innovation Union Competitiveness report, Directorate-General for Research and Innovation, European Union, Brussels http://ec.europa.eu/research/innovation-union/pdf/competitiveness-report/2011/iuc2011-full-report.pdf, accessed: 1/4/2017

Gick, M and Holyoak, K (1980) Analogical problem solving, Cognitive Psychology, Volume 12, Issue 3, July 1980, Pages 306–355

Gordon, W (1961) Synectics the Development of Creative Capacity, Harper and Brothers.

Hippel, E (1994) "Sticky Information" and the Locus of Problem Solving: Implications for Innovation, Management Science, Vol 40, Issue 4, pp. 429 – 439

Hut, R (2017) What are the 10 biggest global challenges? World Economic Forum 2017 Report. https://www.weforum.org/agenda/2016/01/what-are-the-10-biggest-global-challenges/, accessed: 1/4/2017

Jahrami, H and Buheji, M (2012) Reporting a Success Story in the Context of Public Sector: Factors That Matters, Journal of Public Administration and Governance, Vol. 2, No. 3, pp. 96-103

Jonassen D.H. (1997) Instructional design models for well-structured and III-structured problem-solving learning outcomes, Educational Technology Research and Development, Volume 45, Issue1, pp 65–94

Jonassen, D.H. (2000) Toward a design theory of problem solving, Educational Technology Research and Development, Vol 48, Issue 4, pp 63–85

Jonassen, D.H. and Hernandez-Serrano (2002) Case-based reasoning and instructional design: Using stories to support problem solving, Educational Technology Research and Development. June, Volume 50, Issue 2, pp 65–77.

Kendler, Howard H.; Kendler, Tracy S. (1962) Vertical and horizontal processes in problem solving. Psychological Review, Vol 69(1), Jan, pp. 1-16.

Leonard-Barton, D (1995) Wellsprings of Knowledge: Building and Sustaining the Sources of Innovation University of Illinois at Urbana-Champaign's Academy for Entrepreneurial Leadership Historical Research Reference in Entrepreneurship. Available at SSRN: https://ssrn.com/abstract=1496178

Newell and Simon (1972) HUMAN PROBLEM SOLVING, Englewood Cliffs, NJ, Prentice-Hall.

Qin, Z; Johnson, D and Johnson, R (1995) Cooperative Versus Competitive Efforts and Problem Solving, Volume: 65 issue: 2, page(s): 129-143

Sawery, B (1990) Concept Learning versus Problem Solving: Revisited. Journal of Chemical Education, v67 n3 p253-54 Mar

Terwiesch, C and Xu, Y (2008) Innovation Contests, Open Innovation, and Multiagent Problem Solving, Management Science, July, 54:9, pp. 1529-1543

Thrash T. M., Elliot A. J., Maruskin L. A., Cassidy S. E. (2010). Inspiration and the promotion of well-being: tests of causality and mediation. J. Pers. Soc. Psychol. 98, 488–506

Yamauchi T. (2002) The self-organizing consciousness entails additional intervening subsystems Behavioral and Brain Sciences. 25: 360

CHAPTER 2

Shaping the Anatomy of Socio-Economic Community Problems towards Effective Solutions[2]

Introduction

Any socio-economic problem regardless of its nature carries with it default solutions. However, these solutions might not bring-in effective outcome solutions in a way to prevent such a problem not to occur again. i.e. many solutions offered today either they are totally resource-dependent or carry no breakthrough solution that would ensure society development. Kendler et al., (1962).

Therefore, in this chapter review the communities' problems (CPs) and the way they are analysed. Then the capacity inside the socio-economic issues are explored to realise how it demands could be met. The complexity of the socio-economic problems shall be investigated through understanding its anatomy. (Cox, 1995; Wals, 1994; Bull et al.,1988).

Based on the synthesis of the literature review, a framework shall be extracted from a qualitative analysis of the different

---

[2] Buheji, M (2019), Shaping the Anatomy of Socio-Economic Community Problems towards Effective Solutions, **Social Sciences Research Journal,** (7) 1.

socio-economic problems analysed, Jonassen, (2000). The analysis shall help to understand how the problem is dissected in a way that its hidden opportunities are exploited and optimised towards an effective outcome. Buheji (2018b).

Literature Review

Communities Problems

Problems are available in every community as a fact of life. No community regardless of its level of development is free from problems. In fact, any community claims that it does not have problems means it is not developing. However, some communities managed to tackle its issues with a close focus on the socio-economic stability, as Scandinavian Communities, and thus eliminated or mitigated the influence of such problems. Qin et al. (1995).

There are many communities problems that have been tackled by different socio-economic advocates that covered issues as: instability of the community economy, unemployment, theft, security, youth migration, quality of life, adolescent problems, low accessibility to critical survival services and utilities as electricity or clean water, increase in child and women abuse, families instability, crime and violence, domestic violence, drug use, environmental contamination, ethnic conflict, health disparities, HIV/ AIDS, hunger, inadequate emergency services, inequality, jobs, lack of affordable housing, poverty, racism, transportation, extremist control, corruption, low society productivity, etc. This chapter shall try to understand the anatomy of the communities' problems and the best way of eliminating it. This is very important as it foresight the challenges of the communities in future and its high possibilities of being more complicated. Wals (1994); Newell and Simon (1972).

Studies show that communities problem that was analysed carefully or tackled based on observation early are less prone to repeat. Being resource driven to solve might help a community problem (CP) to decline, but will not necessarily help to prevent it from occurring. (Buheji, 2017; Cox, 1995; Bull et al., 1988).

Analysing a Community Problems

Solving communities' problems with appreciated outcome requires good analysis that would lead to better long-run solutions. The CP analysis would need to take into consideration the frequency, the duration of the problem occurrence. How many people are affected or impacted with it? CP should be appreciated in how it is disrupting the community's life, and the possible severity on the stability of the socio-economy. How this CP is creating cultural change or influencing about assumptions, attitudes and mindset about life. (Buheji, 2018a; Davidson and Sternberg, 2003; Bull et al., 1988).

Sometimes an issue is perceived as a CP, but in reality, there are many opportunities of it, or it is an issue that is giving us signs for the greater problem, Buheji (2018b). For example, the issue of more suicides registered in a particular community is a sign for non-ability to control hidden mental health diseases, such as anxiety. The suicide was a sign for us to take care of the lack of anxiety management in the community. Hence, it needs to be ensured when analysing CP why such an issue exists and do that without bias. This means we need to start the analysis after collecting many unbiased observations that can be synthesised and turned into pieces of evidence. Cox (1995).

Any CP should be seen as being the outcome of something; this something is what needs to be discovered. Thus we need to determine the barriers and the resources or the assets associated with CP, Cox (1995). Here we need to investigate what are the opportunities, that sometimes might be represented by the barriers or the obstacles towards a solution that we need to explore and exploit. When we exploit the opportunities in the CP, we could specifically address where to hit or pull, with minimal resources, to come with a problem solution outcome. Buheji (2018b, 2017).

The analysis of the community problem means we could clearly analyse the CP and realise its possible consequences. This means finding opportunities that would give chances for addressing causalities more effectively.

Managing the Capacity vs the Problem Demand

Any CP need cognitive energy that requires modulation (Goldstein and Levin, 1987). Attempting to solve CP need the first development of its recognition through observation that clarifies the problem and creates an analysis of all data and thus developing solutions. This means we need to dissect the problem to the level where we discover its capacity.

When CP solution is planned, it should include till the stage of the validation of the piloted or model solution, or the maintenance of its outcome. Once a CP is recognised the community issue should be clearly defined with precise objectives and impacts. This means understanding the CP environment and the type of capacity that would address its demands. Hence we can focus on symptoms that would enhance the capacity with minimal dependence on extrinsic resources. Cox (1995); Wals, (1994).

One of the sources of discovering the type of CP capacity is through studying the sources of failure frequencies. I.e. having causes for intermittent failures is different that conditional failures. Hence, addressing issues as the CP frequency, duration, range, severity, equity, perception all participate in exploring a problem capacity. For example, knowing and recognising of the rising percentage of the population who are at risk of being patients with Non-Communicable Disease (NCD) during any stage of their lives would lead seeing the capacity in relevance to speed of discovering the NCDs potential patients before they acquire it during any stage of their life. Alternatively, in minimising the period in their life where they would acquire it and or minimising the severity of the NCDs during any stage of their life.

The other way of discovering the CP capacity is to investigate the type of problem mindset, Mayer (1992). i.e. what behaviour, or condition, or attitude it carries. Again one of the outcome solutions for the NCDs is dealing with the attitudes and the behaviours or the mindset. Hence, shaking the assumptions about the lifestyle through working with chronic NCDs families means we raise the capacity for facing the CP. (Buheji, 2018a; Davidson and Sternberg, 2003; D'Zurilla et al.,1971).

Hence, one could conclude that the real cause of a CP may not be immediately apparent. It may be a function of social, economic, or political conditions, or it may be rooted in behaviour or situation that may be manipulated, D'Zurilla et al. (1971). We need to dare to identify the forces that drive the CP. These forces are considered to be the force field analysis. Part of the rising of the CP capacity is to restrain those forces that act to enhance the problem. Example of these forces would be as the social structure, the cultural traditions, the ideology, the lack of knowledge, the lack of accessibility or availability to specific services. Cox (1995).

2.4 Why Socio-Economic Problems are complex?

Most of the socio-economic problems can be characterised as being intransparent, i.e. lack clarity of the situation. For example, most of the socio-economic problems would have unclear constructs about its reason for existence, or transience. The CP complexity is represented in the numbers of constructs that are related or interrelated with it. Even the number of decisions that influence it. Take for example the issue of poverty. Swaminthan (2008); Cox, (1995).

In order to simplify a CP, we need to deal with its dynamics, i.e. how it changes over time. Again here the issue of NCDs is an excellent example as NCD are increasing generation after generation. We also need to investigate what are the constraints and the sensitivity of this CP.

The more CP is real and deep into the society the more it is likely to be complex. Economic development may depend on the global economy; a force you cannot have much effect on. You may have opposition, either from within the community itself, or from powerful forces trying to protect their own interests. Cox (1995).

Socio-Economic Problem Anatomy

It is very hard to change anything in life without understanding its structure and its anatomy. Targeting the anatomy of socio-economic problem help in differentiating the level of understanding of the function of the problem outcome and how its structure can be observed, categorised and then diagnosed. Without understanding the problem anatomy, we cannot realise the story it carries within it. If the case is a complex socio-economic problem, we need to have close analytical views similar to what is done when dissecting the anatomy of that problem. The idea of dissecting the socio-economic problem is to study the most effective ways and approaches that would create the greatest outcome efficiently. Understanding the story of a socio-economic problem build its value-streamed solution or what we call 'outcome'. The clarity of this 'outcome' would help us to create a differentiated change in our lives, besides the lives of our communities. Buheji and Ahmed (2017).

The anatomy of any socio-economic problem is made of two main parts: social problem and economic problem, Buheji

(2018a); Newell and Simon (1972). These two part are inter-related, i.e. they are dependent on each other, i.e. one influence the other. Through understanding the relation of these part and their influence directions, we can catch the threads of breakthrough solutions. For example, having social problems like poverty, illiteracy, corruption, unemployment would lead or be related somehow to economic problems later. Same thing when we have energy crisis, inflations, over-population and unequal income distribution it would be related to social problems later. Once we establish the detailed relationship between the 'social problem' and it 'economic factors' of the socio-economic issue this would mean that we have started to 'dissect' the problem anatomy. Dissecting a problem would help to search and see new approaches to interpreting and experiencing its insights. This would create an excellent environment for breakthrough solutions. Swaminthan (2008).

In certain socio-economic situations, a socio-economic problem is regarded as an unwelcomed, or a serious condition that needs to be dealt with, or managed effectively; dissecting it effectively would ensure its proper elimination most efficiently and effectively. A problem might be due to instability in certain results, or unsustainability of the expected ones, as the issue of the instability in the rates of unemployment in a country.

In certain high achieving cultures, the socio-economic CP start when opportunities are missed, or the resources are limited, or not effectively being utilised. Other culture would see their socio-economic problems start when their community has a low capacity in pursuing innovation, or has been losing initiatives. In certain communities' socio-economic problems found to exist due to the unaligned, or the unattained development, or growth strategies. In many leading countries that as Canada and Scandinavian countries, a CP could be heard when searching for breakthroughs and creating legacy or recording performance. Buheji (2018a), Cox (1995).

Methodology

Based on the literature reviewed, a qualitative evaluation of the CPs would be explored through two types of evaluation tables. The first table would focus on the list sample of communities issues that shape the anatomy of the socio-economic problem. This table links the field visits observations with the opportunities seen. The second table focus on the type of communities issues shaping the socio-economic problems anatomy. i.e. this table links the communities issue with the socio-economic problem.

These two tables would build both the framework of solving socio-economic issues which are called (DARE) and is represented by the first table and then (DISSECT); which is completed by the second table. Based on the framework, some success factors would be proposed to help to set the socio-economic CP's towards a differentiated outcome and a breakthrough solution that develop the community.

Findings

In order to understand how the community problem (CP) practically works in relevant to socio-economic issues, we need to (DISSECT) it as we do in anatomy. This would be done in two stages first through problem realisation stage as synthesised from the literature reviewed and it could be called (DARE). In (DARE) the way field observation brings to the CP is realised through the opportunities discovered for each socio-economic issue presented. Then, we will see how to design community issue outcome from (DISSECTING) the problem and defining its main sources.

Table 1 which represent the DARE part, list sample of communities issues that shape the anatomy of the socio-economic problem. To show practically how opportunities are exploited from CP, five socio-economic issues were selected. The socio-economic

The Defiance

issues vary in background, starting with CP issue shown in the failure to optimise the utilisation of the role of thermal water to the benefit of health tourism in a Bosnian village through its treatment SPA centre services. The other issue, was the quality of life with people with disabilities that managed through NGO's. The third issue was the challenges of 'children of unknown parent' Home-Care centres. The fourth issue taken was discussing the effective outcome of Women-Empowerment associations. The last issue in Table (1) shows how we can exploit the opportunities for a village through their honey and fruit juice factory.

Table 1 shows examples of early observations (called for short 'obs') from the first field visit for the assets, or the barriers, or the resources, or the processes that might influence the socio-economic status of the community in relevant to each issue sampled. The table shows how the observations and the 'hidden opportunities' (called for short 'opp') that build-up the proper information on the problem, to generate potential solutions and outcomes.

Table 1. Relation between Observations and Opportunities that are generated from the Field Visit

Field Visit Observations	Opportunities Seen
Socio-Economic Issue1: No clear value-added contribution for 'Thermal Water Treatment' in the village SPA Services	
Obs 1- Variety of Treatment Specialty Obs 2- Level of Services to be challenged Obs 3- No enough studies to prove the uniqueness of Water Treatment Obs 4- Only 50 % of the treatments use water	Opp 1- Need for compiling the data on cases of Water Treatment effect Opp 2- Need for classification of the conditions of the patients (range, diseases, sex, etc.). Opp 3- Can measure and publish the impact of water treatment Opp 4- The Wealth of 'thermal water' services are not clearly appreciated Opp 5- Improve the ways of packaged services are delivered Opp 6- Many possibilities of sharing- economy in tourist attraction marketing program

Field Visit Observations	Opportunities Seen
Socio-Economic Issue2: Unstable quality of life for People with Disability getting services through NGO's	
Obs 1- Operating cost Obs 2- No evaluation for the type of strengths within the targeted sector	Opp 1- potential investment in people with disabilities Opp 2- Classification for the type of abilities available Opp 3- No trust funds that support such NGO's Opp 4- No measures on tangible results of the services delivered
Socio-Economic Issue3: Children Of Unknown Parent Home Care	
Obs 1- Not clear whether causality of cases is deeply analysed Obs 2- Total dependence on external funds Obs 3- 140 children to the age of 18 Obs 4- No clear followup plans for youth after leaving Home Care Centres	Opp 1-Focus on the three parties for volunteering (financiers, intermediaries, beneficiaries). Opp 2- Potentials for creating Trust for Home Care Opp 3- No efforts for preventing the repeat of cases (i.e. Children with unknown parents) and to prevent the problem from the source Opp 4- Follow-up cases and ensure their total independence & 'leading by example'
Socio-Economic Issue4: Enhancing the level of Women's Empowerment targets through NPOs'	
Obs 1- Focus on the Non-Profit Organisation (NPO) and for Profit Org. Obs 2- Research in the field of women Obs 2- Women empowerment is seen from the services angle only.	Opp 1- Strategic planning and impact measurement focus on basic empowerment through services mainly Opp 2- Re-evaluate type of woman competitiveness training programs and their value towards 'women development' and 'women advancement'.
Socio-Economic Issue5: Improving the villagers' return of honey and fruit juice factory	
Obs 1- Market (Supply vs Demand) Obs 2- Increasing consumer confidence Obs 3- No clear measures to enhance market size & differentiation of product	Opp 1- Research Focus on high-end products supply chain (i.e. honey) Opp 2- Conduct market study to re-packaging, distribution and supply chain of the honey and fruit juice. Opp 2- Diversify the villagers' products using the factories facilities.

Hence, the main part of CP anatomy is to apply DARE table constructs, i.e. to link observations with the 'hidden opportunities' inside the socio-economic problem.

After the field visit observations, one could analyse and synthesis the socio-economic CP. Therefore, DISSECTING the CP can be exploited through Table 2. Table 2 shows that when gathering information about a CP, there are several different methods one could use. It is worth to mention that no one method is better than another and that opportunities exploitation depends on many conditions that surround the socio-economic problem.

Table 2. Type of Communities Issues Shaping the Socio-Economic Problems Anatomy

Community Issue	Example of Socio-Economic Problem
Opportunities are missed	Lack of basic needs in creating safe food
Resources are limited	Stretching of Police Forces to cover the fast demographic development
Resources are not effectively utilised	Lack of effective utilisation of patient beds
Low Innovation Capacity	Reduce the sanitary system blockages that cause diseases and reduce the quality of life.
Loss of Initiatives	Closing the gap and accelerating the transformation towards 'Women Development' instead of 'Women Empowerment' after five years from the Women National Plan Kick-off.
Unaligned, or unattained development or growth strategies	Re-establishing the National University (Research and Development) outcome that would help to deliver better profitable multi-disciplined projects and also inspire effective project closure. Re-alignment of and integration between contracted projects and published papers are achieved.

Community Issue	Example of Socio-Economic Problem
Searching for Breakthroughs & Legacy Creation, or Creating better Record performance	Specifying the qualities of water in the 'Water Treatment Spa' in the specific region of Bosnia rather than treating with water without scientific claim or evidence. This breakthrough niche helped to establish better results in the patients 'length of stay' and enhancing the marketing strategy about the nature of water uniqueness compared to popular Spa competitors in other countries.

Each of these community issues sets the scene for an outcome that would develop the community and address all the CPs once and for all.

Discussion

The study of the CP principles from socio-economic perspectives requires defining and understanding its anatomy. Without the anatomy of such problems, it may not be clear exactly what could be its solution outcome. Defining the problem accurately based on the hidden opportunities seen through its dissected anatomy found to clearly influence the solutions, or even the breakthroughs it can bring to the community. To reach a creative breakthrough problem solution one may sort out the symptoms of the problem from the problem itself. Therefore, it is important to identify the underlying socio-economic problem in order to generate the right solutions and differentiated outcome. Buheji (2017).

Figure (1) illustrates the eights steps that make us move from (DARE) to (DISSECT) in dealing with the socio-economic problem. As shown in Figure (1), CP problem could start counter-clock after setting the intent to discover how to establish the socio-economic problem thinking that would differentiate our communities' development. This could help to establish the socio-economic models through the different 'vectors of wealth' which is a term summarises the assets, or the barriers, or the resources that would bring the problem solution outcome, or explore the 'hidden opportunities'.

These vectors of wealth would help us to start the first attempts in visualising how re-invent the socio-economic stories. Once this early visualisation is done, we can start our journey to understand and dissect the socio-economic CP effectively. At this stage, we can put a design or factors on how to overcome CPs 'mental blocks' and establish its breakthroughs.

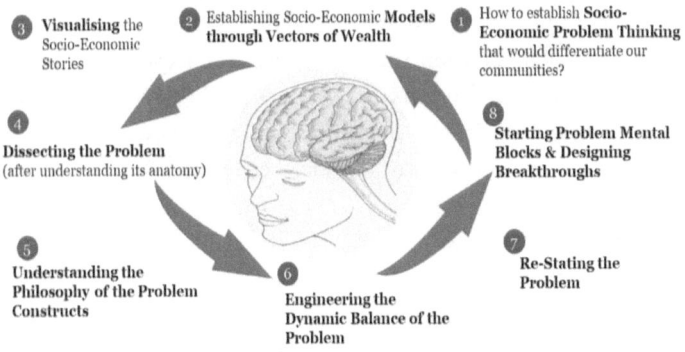

Figure 1. Framework of DARE to DISSECT steps in dealing with Socio-economic CPs.

Conclusion

Taking into account the literature reviewed, the synthesis done in the tables and the framework proposed for dissecting a socio-economic community problem (CP's); a guideline from factors could be proposed that would bring breakthroughs toward an effective community outcome. There are *key success factors* that could be proposed for shaping the anatomy of socio-economic CPs towards these breakthrough of effective solutions.

The first success factor for an effective CP outcome is the problem solution which comes from small projects consisting of several small, accumulated and connected attempts. These attempts help us to explore opportunities within the problem, or what the problem could bring to the organisation, or the community. In summary, this success factor creates a value-added contribution to the targeted socio-economy.

The second success factor retrieved from the discussion is the problem solution which seeks to address the mindset of the socio-economic issue identified. This could be followed by a problem-solution that aims to measure the impact of the outcome proposed on the community. This could be followed by a success factor for the problem-solution that maximises the exploration of CP internal capacities. This, in turn, makes us feel that we can change and appreciate reality, no matter what are the circumstances or the working environment of the socio-economic issue.

References

Buheji, M. (2017). Understanding Problem-Solving in Inspiration Labs. *American Journal of Industrial and Business Management, 7*, 771-784. https://doi.org/10.4236/ajibm.2017.76055

Buheji, M. (2018a). *Re-inventing Our Lives- A Handbook for Socio-Economic Problem Solving.* AuthorHouse, UK.

Buheji, M. (2018b). The Art of Capturing Opportunities— Screening Arab Social Entrepreneurs. *American Journal of Industrial and Business Management, 8*, 803-819. https://doi.org/10.4236/ajibm.2018.84055

Buheji, M., & Ahmed, D. (2017). *Breaking the Shield- Introduction to Inspiration Engineering: Philosophy, Practices and Success Stories.* Archway Publishing, Simon & Schuster, USA.

Bull, J., Cromwell, M., Cwikiel, W., Di Chiro, G., Guarina, J., Rathje, R., Stapp, W., Wals, A. & Youngquist, M. (1988). *Education in Action: A Community Problem Solving Program for Schools*. Thomson-Shore, Dexter, Michigan.

Cox, F. (1995). Community problem solving: A guide to practice with comments. In Rothman, J., Erlich, J., & Tropman, J. (eds.), *Strategies of community intervention* (5th ed., pp. 146-162). Itasca, IL: F. E. Peacock.

Davidson, J., & Sternberg, R (2003). *The Psychology of Problem-solving*, Cambridge University Press. https://doi.org/10.1017/CBO9780511615771

Jonassen, D. H. (2000) Toward a design theory of problem-solving. *Educational Technology Research and Development*, 48(4), 63–85. https://doi.org/10.1007/BF02300500

Kendler, H., Kendler, H., & Tracy, S. (1962). Vertical and horizontal processes in problem-solving. *Psychological Review*, 69(1), 1-16. https://doi.org/10.1037/h0038537

Mayer, R. (1992). Thinking, Problem-solving, Cognition. *A Series of books in psychology* (2nd Ed.). W.H. Freeman & Co Ltd.

Newell and Simon (1972). *Human Problem-Solving*, Englewood Cliffs, NJ, Prentice-Hall.

Qin, Z., Johnson, D., & Johnson, R. (1995). *Cooperative Versus Competitive Efforts and Problem-solving*, 65 (2), 129-143.

Swaminthan, N. (2008). What Do We think When We (Try to) Solve Problems? Scientific American.

Wals, A. (1994). Action Research and Community Problem-solving: environmental education in an inner-city. *Journal of Educational Action Research*, 2(2), 163-182. https://doi.org/10.1080/0965079940020203

Zurilla, D., Thomas J., Goldfried, & Marvin, R. (1971). Problem-solving and behaviour modification. *Journal of Abnormal Psychology*, 78(1), 107-126. https://doi.org/10.1037/h0031360

CHAPTER 3

Application of Differential Diagnose in Inspiration Economy Labs[3]

Introduction

Inspiration has captured and continues to capture the interest of so many cultures and organisations, yet it is just being more clarified in its source of recently by the work of Thrash and Elliott (2004, 2003). As psychologists they and other started to see clearly that inspiration is a status that can be ignited by overcoming challenges and also solving problems.

The world is also in search today for more positive solutions that come from hidden opportunities. Therefore, concepts that help to explore or unleash opportunities are more and more in demand in real life. Differential Diagnosis (DD) is one of the concepts studies and reviewed to see its potential ability to help in this strive for better solutions (Richardon et al., 2005). In searching for an inspiration opportunity, the technique of

---

[3] Buheji, M and Ahmed, D (2016) Application of Differential Diagnose in Inspiration Economy Labs – A LITERATURE REVIEW, **International Journal of Applied Business and Economic Research**,13 (8) 3681-3687, IJER Serials Publications.

observation was discussed by Buheji and Thomas (2016) in the handbook of Inspiration Economy to be the best methodology for unleashing hidden opportunities. With focused observations, specific experiments are identified to answer the hidden questions. In learning from the mystery stories of Sharlek Homes, Hintikka (1983) shows how the observation of facts would result in Homes concluding, for a theft case for example, that the watchdog did not bark as the horse was being stolen. Based on this critical observation, as Hintikka mentioned, Holmes would start an abductive process that leads to questioning 'who is the watchdog trainer?' Moreover, since the stable master is observed to be the owner of the horse, then he would be in the area under question.

The techniques that Sharlek Homes used is more scientifically evidenced today through the DD used by the medical community. Since there is no enough literature review that has covered the application of DD in areas other than diagnosing the patients and narrowing down the problem in relevance to treatment, the following literature review is considered to close a main gap in literature for both researchers and practitioners, especially for those whom are considering to create a change with minimal resources.

Literature Review

Introduction to Differential Diagnosis

DD is a technique first used in medicine to distinguish between a particular disease and condition from others that present similar clinical features (Richardson et al.,2002). With DD techniques physicians are trained during their medical studies to systematically identify the potential presence of a disease where multiple alternatives are possible. Thus, as a professional medical problem-solver they are expected to use a process of elimination that shrinks the «probabilities» of candidate conditions to negligible levels, by using evidence such as symptoms, patient history, and medical knowledge. Thus as professionals with DD, those physicians are trained to take challenges and to come up with more definitive diagnostic checks. Actually, through DD physicians become better forecasters of possibilities and probabilities with more focused evidence gathered to eliminate the unlikely.

Mechanics of Differential Diagnosis

DD is based mainly on four steps: evaluation, calculating the risk factors, setting proper diagnostic criteria and then being open minded for other conditions to consider (Richardson et al., 2002). The DD depends on the depth and the quality of the assessment of symptoms to be considered. For example, the physician is expected to check the severity of breathlessness, cough, sputum production, wheezing, chest tightness, weight loss or anorexia; or the change in alertness or mental status, fatigue, confusion, anxiety, dizziness, pallor or cyanosis, or whether the patient has a chronic cough or sputum production. Hence, DD opens up many possibilities for diagnosis that would help to related and interpolate or even associate between different symptoms.

Also, other observation that DD known to focus on is the medical history of the patient. For example, patients would be checked for their allergies, sinus problems and diseases. Thus DD in medicine has successful case studies in reducing the risk factors and minimising the exposures of the patients whether in the process of diagnosis or interventions.

In order to understand how DD work, let us see how the profound knowledge physician would decide to admit an emergency patient with chest pain problems. The physician would check and evaluate all the data prior to hospitalisations and would ask for vital signs including checking the respiratory rate, pattern, effort and make pulse oximetry. Based on this he/she would start to build an "association" with the situation of the extremities and do an inspection for the chest to see the palpation and percussion of the lungs. Observations as hearing of wheezing, crackles, and decreased breath sounds should part of the holistic diagnosis. Here the final refinement of the decision has to be linked to be pulmonary and not pulmonary. (Richardson et al., 2005).

If the decision to go into pulmonary prognosis then it would focus on potential probabilities of its being asthma, bronchogenic carcinoma, bronchiectasis, tuberculosis, etc. If humans choose to go into non-pulmonary prognosis, then they need to suspect congestive heart failure, Hyperventilation syndrome/panic attacks, vocal cord dysfunction, etc.

Application of Differential Diagnosis for non-medical problem solving

The mechanics of DD can be analogically analysed. In problem-solving and lean thinking, Dr Shrinivas Gondhalekar (called Dr G) from India, whom the researcher was fortunate to work with, is one of the few people that managed to apply DD and even develop its utilisation outside the medical discipline (Gondhalekar and Sheth, 2005). Dr G considered the technique to be unique since it enhances our brain ability to break the logical thinking and use "backwards thinking" instead of the standard problem solving "forward thinking". Dr G experienced that through using the DD, he saw solutions transcends from being based on knowledge to being solid on profound knowledge.

Mohamed Buheji & Dunya Ahmed

Learning from Differentiation Diagnosis and its application in Inspiration Labs

The learning from DD methodology and how it is applied in medicine is that if human want to apply it effectively and make it to a more igniting source for inspiration. Need to start to specify humbly scope of inspiration targeted, by first observing the physical content. Then, the need to start the "Differential Diagnosis" journey that leads to more discovering of opportunities, forecasting and visualisation, as shown in Figure (1).

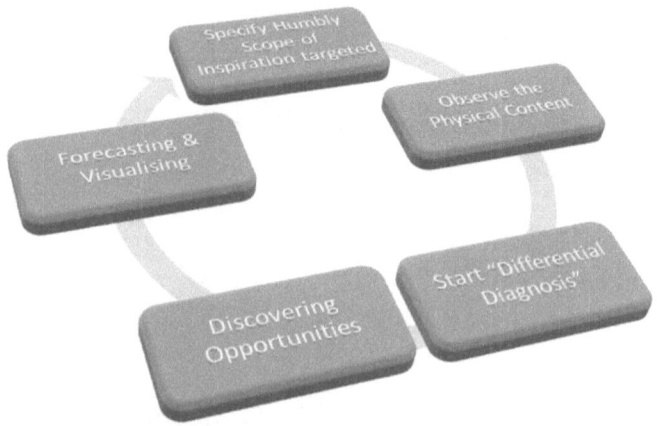

Figure (1) represent the role of Differential Diagnosis in Inspiration Labs Journey

Based on the DD analysis would usually have two main mind map paths, same as the issue was discussed regarding rolling out a prognosis of either the observations lead to a pulmonary or non-pulmonary relate diseases.

Such elimination decisions usually enhance our ability to create more focused observations for unrecognised needs. Continuing in using DD surely raise our curiosity to find hidden opportunities and make us more satisfied with opportunity explored. Differentiation between those who have and have not would lead to more new profound knowledge that enhances our ability to forecast for the future.

Figure (2) represent how Differential Diagnosis would raise our ability

In IE researcher have tried to develop the utilisation of DD to enhance further the capacity of the people ability to observe and improve later the capacity of the organisations to find opportunities without extra resource.

Further Opportunities Discovery through Differential Diagnosis

Hoekzema and Palmer (2005) shown that there are various methods of performing a differential diagnostic procedure, but in general, it is based on the idea that one begins by considering the most common diagnosis first. Only after ruling out the simplest diagnosis should the clinician consider more complex or exotic diagnoses.

Richarson et al. (2002) shown that to discover more opportunities from DD one have to complete the following steps:
1. Need to gather all information about the sample targeted and then create a symptoms list.
2. Lists all possible causes (candidate conditions) for the symptoms.
3. Prioritises the list by placing the most urgently dangerous possible causes at the top of the list.
4. Rules out or treats possible causes, beginning with the most urgently dangerous condition and working down the list. Rule out—practically—means use tests and other scientific methods to determine that a candidate condition has a negligible probability of being the cause.

Then it should remove diagnoses from the list by observing and applying tests that produce different results, depending on which diagnosis is correct.

Application of "Threshold Model" in Inspiration Labs

The "Threshold Model" was developed by Stephen Pauker and Jerome Kassirer in the 1980's. Threshold model provides a framework for self-controlled thinking diagnosis. For example, with Threshold Model can help the DD practitioner to rule out the diagnosis since he/she will know when to stop ordering a test, "rule out" a diagnosis, or even begin a treatment.

The threshold model help us to be independent from our judgement, as it would help each investigator to interpret tests and even act differently in different scenarios. The model is known to challenge evidence-based practice to move from implicit to explicit decision-making.

The threshold scale help to close the gap that faces the investigator usually during DD since it would help to decide on when to start taking a sample and when to start making a judgement for treatment, or explore further opportunities. Figure (3) shows the Threshold Model Scale.

Figure (3) Threshold Model Scale

Hoekzema and Palmer (2005) given examples about how to optimise the use of the scale. For example, depending on the probability known as the scale test which leads to the treatment threshold to be move. So, if the physician has a probability of more than 60% that the patient has the flu, then the diagnosis would be followed directly by treatment. However, if the probability were less than 10%, would no longer worry about it. During the middle of flu season, if the patient comes in possible flu-like symptoms, the "pretest probability" and is about 30%. Hoekzema and Palmer (2005) mentioned that if the pretest probability of 30% (typical in flu season). These values are "post-test probabilities" and depend on three things: the pretest probability, and the sensitivity and specificity of the test.

Differential Diagnosis and Pull Thinking

Dr G in his book Chronicles of a Quality Detective mentioned about the importance of comparing the results between two samples. He focused on how comparative analysis mindset would be very for DD journey. Through DD pull thinking mindset Dr

G emphasised that the power of ignorance supersedes the power of knowledge, if it manages to challenge the mindset humbly to see the opportunities in a problem from different angles.

Differential Diagnosis as a Dynamic Process

Richardson et al. (2005) seen that DD is a very dynamic process which is based on an intuitive style of thinking. DD found to begin at the onset of the sample presentation directing further questioning, examination, and diagnostic testing. Understanding the utilisation of DD in inspiration labs help to create a more unstructured approach that is continuously evolving towards finding and exploring opportunities.

Conclusion

DD as a technique found to help investigators to challenge facts and actually renew available knowledge. This literature review shows that the scope of the problem (or prefer to call it challenge) under investigators would define the entire journey.

The implementation of DD, outside medical discipline, found to raise the curiosity and create a positive spirit of finding solutions or exploring more opportunities by making people more involved. This technique found to be highly useful for inspiration labs since it would further raise the ability to find suitable observations and exploring more new opportunities.

Reference

Buheji, M and Thomas, B (2016) Handbook of Inspiration Economy. Bookboon.com, ISBN 978-87-403-1318-5.

Buheji, M (2016) Inspiring Governments. LAP LAMBERT Academic Publishing.

Buheji, M; Saif, Z, Jahrami, H (2014) Why Inspiration Matters? Journal of Inspiration Economy, Vol 1, Issue 1, Sep 2014.

Celli BR, MacNee W (2004) Standards for the diagnosis and treatment of patients with COPD: a summary of the ATS/ERS position paper. Eur Respir J; 23:932.

Gondhalkar, S and Sheth, P (2005) Chronicles of a Quality Detective, Indus Source Business Books.

Hoekzema, G and Palmer, E (2015) Mercy Family Medicine Residency, St. Louis, http://documentslide.com/documents/copd-differential-diagnosis-grant-hoekzema-md-program-director-mercy-family-medicine-residency-st-louis-mo-elissa-j-palmer-md-faafp-professor.html Accessed on: 10/10/2016

Richardson, W; Wilson, M; Lijmer, J; Guyatt, G and Cook, D (2002) Differential Diagnosis, American Medical Association.

Thrash, T. M., and Elliot, A. J. (2003). Inspiration as a psychological construct. Journal of Personality and Social Psychology 84, 871. doi: 10.1037/0022-3514.84.4.871.

Thrash, T. M., and Elliot, A. J. (2004). Inspiration: core characteristics, component processes, antecedents, and function. Journal of personality and social psychology 87, 957-973. doi: 10.1037/0022-3514.87.6.957.

Thrash, T. M., Elliot, A. J., Maruskin, L. A., and Cassidy, S. E. (2010). Inspiration and the promotion of well-being: Tests of causality and mediation. Journal of Personality and Social Psychology 98, 488-506. doi: 10.1037/a0017906

CHAPTER 4

Understanding the Economics of Problem-Solving "A Longitudinal Review of the Economic Influence of Inspiration Labs- Three Years Journey on Socio-Economic Solutions[4]

Introduction

Imagine the world if we were able to double, triple, or even quadruple the number of problem solvers, the diversity of solutions, and the scale of social impacts. Imagine if every government and primary private sector opened up their toughest socio-economic challenges, or problems and directed their resources for many problem solvers and the social enterprises.

---

[4] Buheji, M (2019) Understanding the Economics of Problem-Solving "A Longitudinal Review of the Economic Influence of Inspiration Labs- Three Years Journey on Socio-Economic Solutions. **American Journal of Economics**, 9(2): 79-85.

Imagine how innovations would spread across the world would be and how we could tackle most complex problems in more inspiring outcomes. Buheji (2018 a, b) and Eggers and Macmillan (2013 a, b).

We live in a creative world where many of us want to bring solutions to common world problems voluntarily. Therefore, the most resilient economy is the economy that would make such problem-solving economy grows to fill the spaces within this economy. The most resilient economy is the economy that would open the doors for creativity and would encourage the local small and medium businesses to embrace these solutions attempts.

Literature Review

1 The Solution Economy

Solution economy, is a term developed by Eggers and Macmillan (2013 a) to solve the social problems from a multidisciplinary perspective which brings together different background practitioners from businesses, governments, philanthropy and social enterprises to tackle holistically a socio-economic challenge or problem that would serve many stakeholders or beneficiaries.

2 Solving Socio-Economic Problems through Inspiration Labs

Inspiration labs were developed by the research, as part of an international project called Inspiration Economy, over three years ago, to tack socio-economic problems in a disruptive way through identifying first the problem vectors. The problem vectors exploit the opportunities out of the problem. The problem vectors help to tackle the problem effectively and ensure it has both economic and social impact. Buheji (2018a, b, c) and Buheji (2019a, b, c, d).

3 Acceleration of Solution Economy

Solution economy target to accelerate the growing economies and help the problem solvers to support the government in achieving faster delivery of outcome-based solutions. These outcome-driven solutions are critical as governments are shrinking in size and NGO's and Non-profit organisation are doubling in many countries. European Business Review (2016).

Nyarko (2005) seen that knowledge can be captured through problem-solving. The capacity to capture knowledge through problems differentiate the competitive status for nations, or community and help them to master problems associated productivity. Thus, communities can improve their economic productivity and learn to produce new goods by observing how other communities are solving their problems and selectively transfer part of the solution to national problems.

4 Visualising the Economics of Problem-solving and Solution Economy

With problem-solving, solutions economy could help to open up services that meet the citizens' choice, thus shifting the focus from results to the outcome. This help to thrive the socio-economic development efforts of any community. Visualising the economics of problem-solving help governments to provide room for creativity and differentiate their capacity in the delivery of social outcome.

For example, if governments understand the economic return of solving the socio-economic problem, as the problem of Waste Pickers NGO's they could be part of the transformation happening in India's waste management program. The economy of the vectors of such problem comes from the increased demand of the middle class for organised, effective waste and environmental services management. These demands ensure innovative products and services that would guarantee the quality of life of all the beneficiaries in India and would help to enhance the economic return of such initiatives for recycling and eco-friendly projects. However, the government's need to be willing to have more accessibility to important data for its partners that would differentiate its outcomes. The more government provide and collaborate on knowledge sharing the more we would witness a different solution economy that would also create a cultural transformation. Buheji (2018 a, b, c).

5 Issues of Problem-solving Solutions Economy

Problem-solving and solution economy could be applied to any organisation, be it government, NGO's or private sector. However, we would witness the significant differentiation of this economy in chronic complex issues such as poverty, hunger, unemployment, environmental management and youth migration, for example. Hussain (2013).

Usually, the best economic solutions can inspire all type of sectors: business, government, philanthropic and social enterprises. Their currency of inspiration creates a primary value-added outcome. Hence, the benefit of problem-solving and solutions economy is that it would break the bureaucratic boundaries between the three major productivity sectors which means bringing in direct trillions of dollars in social benefits and commercial value, besides tremendous goodwill value.

Design innovative new solutions could be the norm of future economies, where solutions would integrate low-cost health care with fighting poverty-related diseases. Thus, it is an economy where we could expect more solutions that would create markets for social goods and trade solutions instead of dollars to fill what citizens need.

In recent years, an entire economy of societal problem solvers has emerged to tackle old problems in new ways. A rapidly growing and evolving solution economy now focus on social impact currency that if compared to the real value it would convert to millions. Hussain (2013).

6 How Can Solution Economy Solve Bigger Economic Problems?

Christensen (2015) seen that solution economy is like a 'solution revolution' where governments are now tackling complex problems such as climate change, poverty and crumbling infrastructure through more partners. This collaborative economic practice could close the existing gap between government performance and citizen expectations, as it is improving 'solution orientation'.

Seattle's FareStart is an excellent example of economic problems. This catering company and restaurant are staffed by cooks hired through a job placement program. It has flourished, supporting the delivery of more than five million meals to the disadvantaged. They also launched a café to train young baristas, combating the city's high rates of youth unemployment and homelessness.

Eggers and Macmillan (2013a) mentioned that significant enterprises, like Unilever, can be work on solution economy as market innovators, who are committed to addressing unmet community or consumer needs. For example, Unilever started to introduce products, that as soap, that target to meet the needs of people under poverty lines in countries in India and Africa. This initiative integrates both empowerment of entrepreneurs in rural India and increasing awareness of the importance of hand-washing, with an end goal of reducing infant mortality.

Another example that Eggers and Macmillan mentioned for solution economy was Safaricom. Safaricom is leading integrated communications companies in Africa started a project that closes the gap of the enormous percentage of Kenyans who did not have access to banking in any form. By introducing Safaricom

M-Pesa mobile banking phone app, 17 million Kenyans now can conduct business, receive entitlement payments and financial services. Another type of economic solution come from projects like Recyclebank. Such banks help to increase recycling rates by partnering with recycling bin maker and creating business incentivise recycling. The households, in the neighbourhoods in which Recyclebank operates, have recycling bins equipped with a chip that weighs the goods in the bin. Recyclebank credits the households account with points that can be spent on discounts offered by the network of business that Recyclebank has partnered with. This raised recycling rates into rates reached 90%. Hussain (2013). Hence, such sizeable private sector organisations can work on tackling social problems and bring in many goodwill values for the community concerned beside the organisation.

7 Solution Economy vs Economics of Problem Solution

Through partnerships between governments and different problem-solving players; key insights to outcome measurement can enhance the effectiveness of solutions and address more societal challenges. Thus, the solution economy could focus on integrating problem solvers and non-governmental contributors to bring in unique resources and creativity that would address the gap in societal needs. Usually, such problem solvers use disruptive approaches and value exchange solutions.

Economics of problem-solving in Inspiration Labs focus on inspiration currency too. This help to create a differentiated socio-economic outcome. Solution economy also focuses on impact currencies which also based on 'value creation' that enhances the social impact.

Inspiration economy targets, in different ways, to create a transformation in communities through unique approaches of socio-economic solutions and redefining how complex issues could be solved, without extra or with minimal resources. Thus, inspiration economy is similar to solution economy which addresses societal problems, but through disruptive problem-solving that bring opportunities out of the problems, but not necessarily try to create a partnership between government and other sectors. In the solution economy, the economic value is created around the real problems considered to be sources of economic failures.

8 Cycle of Economy Thinking and Problem-solving

Eggers and Macmillan (2013) mentioned about the new cadre of problem-solvers that are changing the global economy. Such problem solvers work on making societies face economic problems, which starts with facing how to make the best use of limited or scarce resources. The economic problem exists because, although the needs and wants of people are endless, the resources available to satisfy the needs and the wants are limited.

Socio-economic problem thinking in inspiration labs help to create the main economic drivers that lead to practical solutions: goal setting, the relationship between problem-solving and capacity development, opportunity management, innovation behaviours, curiosity and rewards, performance improvement and reflections, as shown in Figure (1).

Figure (1) Cycle of Economic Thinking

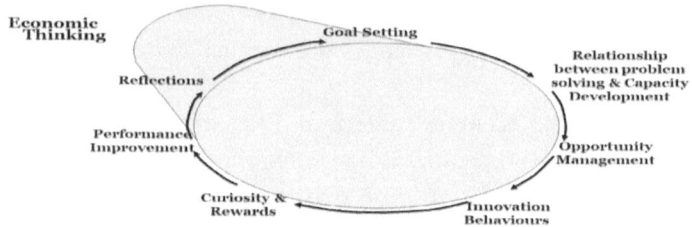

Assessing and re-inventing socio-economic issues can start through understanding the pattern of such problems and its role in the economic structure. Realising problem structure starts with setting up the problem activity profile that links between 1) the type of practices towards establishing problem vectors, 2) access problem vectors, as what are the socioeconomic constructs along with implementation, monitoring and evaluation of the model solution, 3) analysis of problem factors and trends.

Assessing the economics of problem-solving makes us investigate the opportunity of what are the socioeconomic constructs, the possible solution modelling and the implementation, the monitoring, the evaluation of the model solution.

Methodology

In order to investigate the economics of problems solving through the three years experiential learning of the inspiration labs, eight case studies are reviewed for their problem vectors. Then, the analysis of this review is discussed and synthesised in relevance to literature. A proposed framework of the economic constructs or vectors of the socio-economic problems, then set up to the best way for diagnosing the economic problem outcome is presented.

Case Study

1 Role of Problem-solving Case Studies in the Economy

Any economy is a tool for solving the mysteries of the problem investigated. This means that the economy helps us to build our ability for innovative behaviour, capacity for appreciating the opportunity recognition, having a variety of approaches to the economic problem and conflict mitigation and representation.

Since economics is a "social science" the economy of problem-solving starts with seeing the gaps in the inconsistent assumptions, in order to enhance the abundance in solving problems using limited resources. Such problem economics is usually concerned with the problem of using 'scarce resources' to solve communities' problems, or its challenges; such as re-focusing on means of producing (P1), attaining the greatest or maximum fulfilment (P2) and addressing society's unlimited wants (P3).

Based on the field visits and the profound observations, 'opportunities management' can enhance the problem outcome through problem scenario and storyboard, data collection, opportunities and ideas; till solutions are proposed. The influence on the economy starts with a methodology for exploring solutions and determining symptoms and specifications of the problem. Then, exploration of problem opportunities would work on building a story-line that would finalise the socio-economic outcome.

The five constructs of economic solutions engineering economics are about observing the world with genuine curiosity and admitting it is full of mysteries. Then, by trying to solve those mysteries in ways that fit the human behaviour design, we can direct it towards a common purpose. Engineering solutions for problems and challenges can help to visualise solutions, ways of thinking, psychology and exploration questions.

Economics of problem-solving bring in alternatives for managing conflict representations through constructs of observation (what is the essence of the problem?), exploration (depth of problem opportunities), prioritisation (seen and hidden opportunities), mindset (assumptions and behavioural change) and practices that (create models of Opportunities). Since economics is the 'study' of mankind needs, in the 'ordinary business of life', as Alfred Marshall mentioned we then to observe, absorb, apply, analyse and evaluate, create and reflect.

2 Case Studies that reflect the Economic Influence of Problem-solving

The following cases represent the experience of the researcher in exploring economic constructs (called problem vectors) that influence the economic and socio-economic

Case 1- Problem Vectors of Poverty Elimination

In order to manage the economics of problem-solving of poverty alleviation and elimination, we need to utilise and optimise the demographics of the humanitarian stakeholders and where the humanitarian NGO realise their role to be moving people out of poverty and not only making people cope with poverty, as shown in Figure (2).

Figure (2) Illustrates Vectors of Poverty Elimination

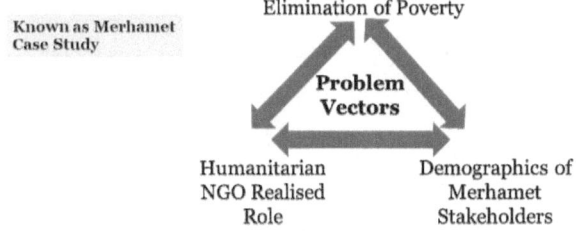

Case 2- Problem Vectors of Prioritising Emergency Beds Case Study

In this case, the target is to manage the economics of problem-solving for prioritising emergency cases and the provision of the related beds for such cases, while also improving patients' clinical management and patients' satisfaction. The solution can be improved through hospitality services management of beds and services, as shown in Figure (3).

Figure (3) Illustrates Vectors of Prioritising Emergency Cases Beds

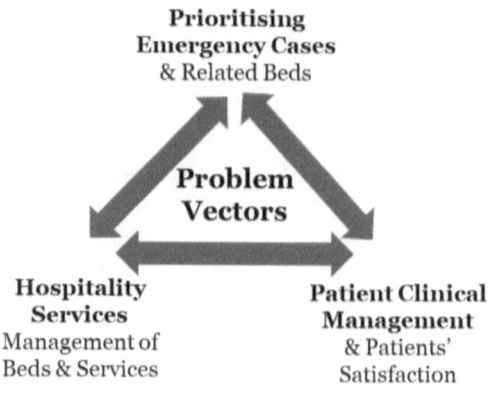

Case 3- Problem Vectors of Fisheries Case Study

In order to manage the economics of problem-solving for improving marine life, we need to improve the vector of fisheries sustainable competitiveness. These vectors also need citizens and consumers' quality of food, as shown in Figure (4).

Figure (4) Illustrate Vectors of Fisheries Improvement

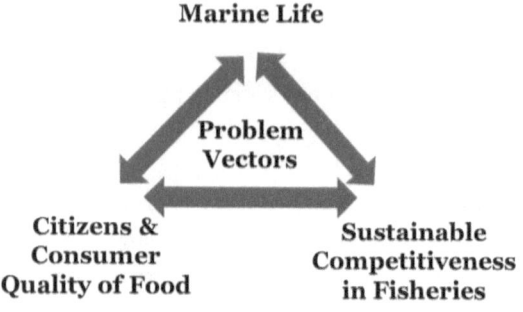

Case 4- Problem Vectors of Reducing Jewellery Theft

Building and maintaining trust in the economy is significant for both consumers and investors. Therefore, for example, there is a significant role for community policing in the prevention of Jewellery Shops. There is an economic value for establishing an incident management system in all Jewellery Shops, besides having prevention through a collaborative community program, as shown in Figure (5).

Figure (5) Illustrates Vectors of Economic Stability & Jewellery Shops Improvement

Case 5- Problem Vectors of Sanitary Blockage Case Study

One of the most critical factors for any country quality of life is the sanitary system. Therefore, the quality of the network design needs to be aligned with the type of socio-economic activities to avoid an adverse effect on the economy. To reduce the problem, the vector of the black spots management system is used to show the effectiveness of predictive maintenance and the role of collaborative community prevention in creating a better socio-economic outcome, as shown in Figure (6).

Figure (6) Illustrates Vectors of the Economics of Sanitary Blockage Solution

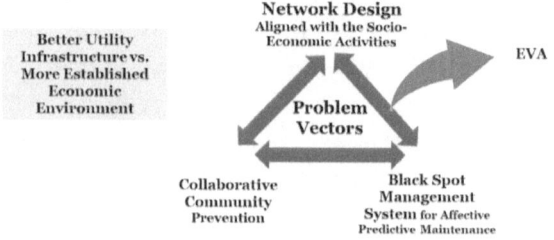

Case 6- Problem Vectors of Anxiety Management Case Study

Anxiety is known to be the cause of deteriorating 'Quality of Life' which affect the socio-economic productivity of any country. Thus the economics of problem-solving focus on reducing the negative influence of chronic anxiety disease through early detection of anxiety. This means we need a communication plan for the related causes and disorders, or anxiety mismanagement in collaboration with partners. Therefore, one of the economics of the solution is to simplify anxiety (self-assessment), as shown in Figure (7).

Figure (7) Illustrates the Vectors of the Economics of Anxiety Management Solution

Case 7- Problem Vectors of Water Leakage Elimination

The economics of solving a significant water loss in countries where water is rare is very obvious. Therefore, an intelligent prediction of water leakage (seen and hidden leakage) and innovation to improve water delivery help to improve the economics constructs of the solution. Therefore, as shown in Figure (8) type of connections, challenges per area water loss and design improvements of water pipes were set as part of the problem solution. Realising sources of water loss, i.e. codifying losses between water desalination stations and consumers' delivery points were set as part of the problem solution plan too.

Figure (8) Illustrates Vectors of the Economics of Sanitary Blockage Solution

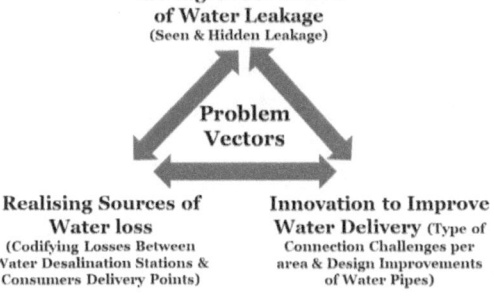

Discussion

1 The Economic Constructs of Socio-Economic Problems

Reviewing the scarce literature and the eight cases that represent the summary of some of the problems solved by inspiration labs, show that the economics of problem-solution lies at the heart of economics. The techniques developed from the need to solve fundamental socio-economic problems facing all community while also ensuring optimisation of productive resources.

Synthesis of all the cases shows there are three repeated constructs of any socio-economic problem-solving experience: 1-understanding the world, 2-understanding the relation of things, 3-understanding the human side. Figure (9) represents the economic constructs that might be part of any problem-solving.

Figure (9) Illustrates the Vectors and Constructs of any Socio-economic Problem

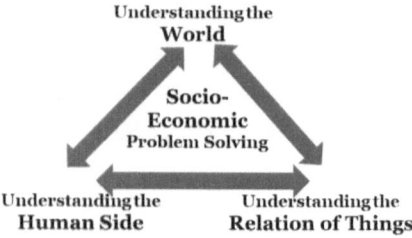

2 Diagnosis of Economic Problem-solving Outcomes

Diagnosis of problem outcome till the stage of discovery has its influence on the economic and the socio-economic status, especially when studying the relation of (area of problems vs area of diagnosis). As we move to an unknown and unclear area on this relation, we experience more area of socio-economic discovery thus more realisation about the problem solution and unlearning of any obstacles that would usually prevent us from making a high economic value solution, as shown in Figure (10).

Figure (10) Illustrates the best area for a Socio-economic Problem Discovery

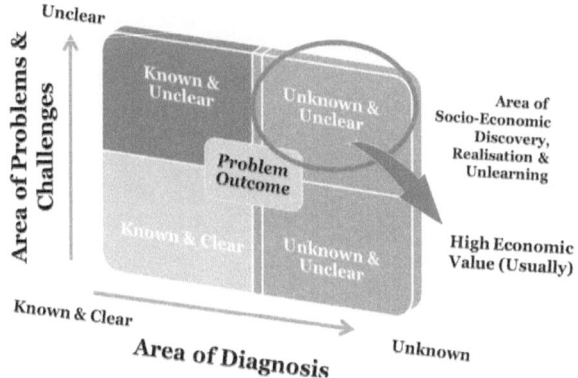

3 Economic Outcome Differentiation through Empathetic Story Scenario

Reviewing all the eight cases presented one could see the empathetic scenario used to create a compelling story with a clear economic outcome. Synthesis of these cases shows that what creates an economic outcome is the complete problem-solving cycle the differentiation that relates from the two directions: the scenario of the problem and its story, with the exploration efforts for problem opportunities. The relation of these two, as shown in Figure (11), i.e. the story visualised and the exploration efforts, help us to generate economically focused facts and ideas that can be identified and consolidated with specific learning areas in relevant to the problem solved.

Figure (11) Illustrates the Cycle Differentiation of the Socio-economic Outcome

Conclusion

This chapter addresses a rare issue in the literature which shows the importance of problem-solving on the economy and the socio-economy. Despite there is not yet clear evidence of the relation between the problem vectors and the scenario of the problem story, the chapter shows the repeated economic trend found from the inspiration labs in all the types of the problem solved. The economic effectiveness of understanding the world of the problem and the relation of things in the relevance of its human side is now clearly illustrated. Using the economics of problem-solving can help to spread the competition of solving socio-economic problems between problem solvers, innovating governments and private enterprises.

References

Buheji, M (2019a) Influence of visualised reflection on 'solving socio-economic problems' – a case from youth economy forums, Int. J. Innovation and Learning, 25 (1), pp. 1-16.

https://www.indersciencconline.com/doi/abs/10.1504/IJIL.2019.096537

Buheji, M (2019b) Shaping the Anatomy of Socio-Economic Community Problems towards Effective Solutions, Issues in Social Science, Vol. 7, No. 1, pp. 1-11. http://www.macrothink.org/journal/index.php/iss/article/view/14524/11461

Buheji, M (2019c) 'The Trust Project' Building better accessibility to Healthcare Services through Behavioural Economics and Inspiration Labs, International Journal of Economics, Commerce and Management, United Kingdom, Vol. VII, Issue 2, February.

http://ijecm.co.uk/wp-content/uploads/2019/02/7234.pdf

Buheji, M (2019d) 'Re-designing the Economic Discovery of Wealth' a Framework for Dealing with the Issue of Poverty, International Journal of Economics, Commerce and Management United Kingdom Vol. VII, Issue 2, February. http://ijecm.co.uk/wp-content/uploads/2019/02/7223.pdf

Buheji, M. (2018a) Re-Inventing Our Lives, A Handbook for Socio-Economic "Problem-Solving", AuthorHouse, UK. https://www.authorhouse.com/Bookstore/BookDetail.aspx?Book=785548

Buheji, M. (2018b) Recognising Lives around Socio-Economies? – Foreword, International Journal of Inspiration & Resilience Economy, 2(2): 0-0

http://article.sapub.org/10.5923.j.ijire.20180202.00.html

Buheji, M. and Ahmed, D (2018c) Understanding Inspiration Currencies in Woman Development Programs, American Journal of Economics, 8(3): 174-182. http://article.sapub.org/10.5923.j.economics.20180803.07.html

Buheji, M (2018d) Nudge Theory vs Inspiration Economy Labs- Comparing the Depth of Influence on Socio-Economics Behaviours, American Journal of Economics; Vol. 8, No.3: 146-154. file:///C:/Users/hp/Downloads/10.5923.j.economics.20180803.04.pdf

Buheji, M (2018e) Practices of Future Foresight in Management of Non-Communicable Diseases -An Early Attempt towards Focusing on 'Foresight Economy' Labs. Advances in Social Sciences Research Journal. Vol.5, No.4, pp. 344-355. http://scholarpublishing.org/index.php/ASSRJ/article/view/4490

Buheji, M. (2018f) Role of Empathetic Engineering in Building More Resilient Green Economy. Case Study on Creating Resilient Self

Sufficient Food Security Programs in the Middle East. Advances in Social Sciences Research Journal, 5(3) 148-157. http://scholarpublishing.org/index.php/ASSRJ/article/view/4280

Buheji, M. (2017a) Understanding Mechanisms of Resilience Economy- Live Application on a Complex Business Model. Advances in Social Sciences Research Journal, 4(14), pp. 52-64. http://scholarpublishing.org/index.php/ASSRJ/article/view/3484/1977

Buheji, M (2017b) Understanding Problem-solving in Inspiration Labs, American Journal of Industrial and Business Management, 7, pp. 771-784, http://file.scirp.org/pdf/AJIBM_2017062216580094.pdf

Christensen, K (2015) How solution economy can solve bigger economic problems? Forbes, Mar 25, http://www.forbesindia.com/article/rotman/how-solution-economy-can-solve-bigger-economic-problems/39735/1

Eggers, W and Macmillan, P (2013a) The Solution Revolution: How Business, Government, and Social Enterprises Are Teaming Up to Solve Society's Toughest Problems. Harvard Business Review Press

Eggers, W and Macmillan, P (2013b) The Solution Economy, Deloitte Global Services Limited. Fast Company. https://www.fastcompany.com/3017461/welcome-to-the-solution-economy

European Business Review (2016) The Solution Economy, http://www.europeanbusinessreview.com/the-solution-economy-a-new-way-to-solve-social-problems/

Hussain, A (2013) The Solution Economy: Problem-solving Everyone Can Agree On. *Roosevelt Institute.* http://rooseveltinstitute.org/millennial-pulsesolution-economy-problem-solving-everyone-can-agree/

Nyarko, Y (2005) Economic Development as Problem-solving, Researchgate

PART TWO
DEFIANT CASE STUDIES

CHAPTER 5

Influencing without Power" Currency in Inspiration Labs: A Case Study of Hospital Emergency Beds[5]

Introduction

While Kendrick (2012) focused on desired behaviours, IE focus on way of implementation to change behaviours. However, Hogg and Cooper (2007) focused on what happens in diversified communities, or people with different backgrounds, multi-discipline and different interest.

When reading currently available literature about Influencing without Power' (IWP), or authority, or resources; it is scarce to hear the word capacity, and rather tend to see the word skills and competency (Probst, 2017). This gap was addressed with the recent literature that came from the projects of IE which focused on 'IWP' that leads to raising the capacity vs demand. So here,

---

[5] Buheji, M (2018) "Influencing without Power" Currency in Inspiration Labs—A Case Study of Hospital Emergency Beds, **American Journal of Industrial and Business Management** 08(02):207-220

it is not only about influencing a project team, or developing skills, or influencing fellow employees; it is much beyond that. It is about an influence that creates an outcome, and that leads to the legacy which means realising actual sustained change into the socio-economy, (Cohen, and Bradford, 2005; Gottwald, 2008).

In the coming sections the author reviews among the huge literature what influence means on the society, i.e. beyond the personal influence which is the focus of most of the literature so far. Ways of influence to the extent of leaving a significant sustained change, called in this chapter legacy is also presented. The importance of 'influencing with power' as a concept and a mindset and especially in instable socio-economies today are discussed.

What does influence mean?

Real influence provokes change. Influence is only valuable when it provokes change in how people operate and think; when it inspires them to take the required action (Vora, 2013).

Influence is more about reciprocity (give and take) between you and another person(s) or between organisations and communities which enables change to happen or attitudes, opinions, or behaviours to be reinforced as per Cohen and Bradford (Cohen, and Bradford, 2005).

Johnson (2008) mentioned about the influence that is built on gaining access to resources needed to be carried out by outstanding efforts. For example, gaining access to resources needed with minimal investment of efforts, using more sound pieces of evidence. Johnson that influence clearly happens when doors swing open freely to those key players whose cooperation needed most. That time we will feel we have achieved central purpose while catalysing valuable change for the targeted community.

Ways to Influence

Lauren Johnson (2008) mentioned about 8 R's as eight ways to create an 'influence without power'. These eight R's start with Reasons, Research, Resonance, Repetition, Resources, Rewards, Real-world events and Resistance. While Linda Hill (1994) seen that there are mainly only two ways to influence without power that is empowering others and cultivating networks.

Buheji and Thomas (2016) defined how to create an influence by four I's. The first I is about individualised personal attention to others, making each individual feel uniquely valued. The second I is about intellectual stimulation where people are actively encouraged to a new look at old methods, to stimulate their creativity and encourages others to look at problems and issues in a new way. The third I is about inspirational motivation where people optimism increased through enthusiasm for possibilities not previously considered. The last and fourth I is about idealised influence where a sense of purpose build more trust and confidence from followers.

Why 'Influencing Without Power' is essential today?

IWP found to create more impact and lasting effect in relevance to socio-economic problems as poverty, low aspirations, QoL, youth demands, social and political instability, low productivity, business instability and issues of migrations. Influencing with minimal resources and without using any official power people would be more committed to creating more differentiated results and outcomes compared to what is expected (Cohen, and Bradford, 2005). Buheji and Thomas (2016) mentioned about more demand being more frequent waves of innovation and with the spread of unstable coexistence or resilience, IWP and with minimal resources can create more differentiation for communities' outcomes.

IWP is highly needed as both a principle of life and mindset, as it enhances survival and competency chances in a very turbulent socio-economy such as it is more witnessed today.

Examples of 'Influence without Power' – from School of Gandhi.

Vora (2013) mentioned about the secret of Mahatma Gandhi 'influence without power' which can be summarised in one word 'simplicity'. Gandhi was independent of all the influence resources, i.e. the position, the wealth, the power and the authority. Yet, Gandhi influenced the whole empire and influenced the hearts, spirit and minds of so many people across the world more than 80 years now.

Vora confirms that Gandhi simplicity confirms that no matter who you are, or where you are in the order, you can make a difference. Gandhi as per Vora worked with others and through them to achieve his objectives, but he never compromised on his own principles. Actually, as per Vora, these principles were the substance that Gandhi generated his influence on others. Therefore, one could summarise that having real accomplishments, experiences, passion and credibility were the real formula of Gandhi's sustained influence. This formula raised people trust on Gandhi, and thus it became one of his influence currencies.

Gandhi also used other way of trust, i.e. trusting people around him. Gandhi knew that when people get trusted, they get influenced as they change when they feel being trusted.

Barriers to 'Influencing without Power'

There are many types of barriers to effective influencing. Most important barriers, however, are relevant to organisational culture. Hierarchical communications and styles tend to prohibit influencing without authority. Studies show product or service complexity control the level of learning that can be done and thus inhibits the ability to influence (Gottwald, 2008; Probst, 2017). Limitation of time dedicated to discovery also found to inhibit people from seeing and verifying the requirements of type of reflection and thus affecting their participation. With the lack of people participation or inconsistent participation, it is hard to 'influence without power'. Hence by employing a consultative approach, project professionals can gain the needed influence to facilitate positive project outcomes.

Research Method

The method in this study consists of an analysis of initiatives carried in one of the largest government hospitals, which needed to explore a change without extra resources or authority. Therefore, a focused IWP research is carried out in-depth followed by a proposed model from IE and labs is presented. Then a case Study of secondary care regional hospital was selected to explore the 'influence without power' currency. Then a comparative analysis is done in the discussion and conclusion. The identity of the hospital is protected due to a contractual agreement about the sensitivity of the issue socio-politically.

The Proposed Model

Based on the experimental theories that were developed from IE and inspiration engineering a model for IWP or with minimal resources is proposed. The following sections explain the theoretical background of the model and its constructs.

'Influencing Without Power' as a type of Inspiration Currency

Cohen and Bradford (2005) proposed a model that reflects how to influence creates currencies. The Cohen-Bradford saw that IWP creates inspiration for building a vision, excellence, morality/ethics. Through such influence currencies human build tasks for resources, information, assistance and support. With influence currencies, human build a type of inspiration currencies as position advancement, recognition, visibility, reputation, networks/contacts and appreciate the importance of insiderness. Also, Cohen and Bradford (2005) seen that relationship built on acceptance, personal support, understanding, and inclusion help people to see self-concept, feel the importance of managing together challenges, with ownership, gratitude and more involvement with reality. (Buheji and Ahmed, 2017).

Why is 'Influence' important for Inspiration Economy for solutions?

IE is about the ability to create positive socio-economic change through utilising the intrinsic powers of the individuals, the organisations and the communities. Once intrinsic powers can be utilised, then the organisation can use these powers to influence a change with being more independent from the resources. This needs first a ready mindset that appreciates the importance of this change. Influencing the mindset make organisations, and communities get more engaged to create a focused outcome towards a targeted legacy (Hogg and Cooper, 2007; Mathieu et al., 2000). The level of influence is significant for inspiration based economy solutions, as without such level of influencing people cannot see how inspiration would leave an impact on the economy and the socio-economy (Buheji and Thomas, 2016; Buheji and Ahmed, 2017).

In today busy life human needs to influence with minimal resources and the quick impact that can be felt by more people. When human prove that they can influence, even if they do not have the power on others, this means human minimise the excuses. Actually, as per Johnson (2008), people will not interact enough unless they stop procrastinating, or stop hesitating, or stop having the feeling that they do not have the power, or the authority, or the resources to influence a change. With the increasing rapidity of technological change and shortening of products/services life cycles that are making the competition more intense, IWP is very important to attract their attention and to utilise the failures, the challenges and turns them to sources of inspiration which researchers call opportunities. Hence, in inspiration based economy IWP is part ofproblem-solving and problem finding that leads to overcome complexity and creation of development.

Figure (1) shows how inspiration engineering labs create different currencies as IWP, inspired mindsets, IC and LLL that create a sustained legacy which shows the importance of IE.

Figure (1) Illustrate the different influences generated by IE mechanisms

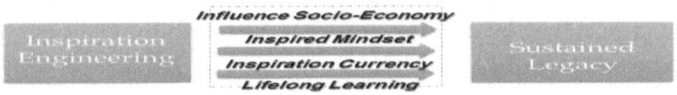

Inspiration Labs Influence

Inspiration labs are considered to be a technique where people are brought together to explore and collect field observations about a specific chronic, or complex or challenging problems and then explore further how to turn it into opportunities, as illustrated in Figure (2). Inspiration labs are therefore considered to be a source of mindset influence, (Buheji and Thomas, 2016; Buheji and Ahmed, 2017). The more human manage to influence others, the more human own the currency to change them, or at least create in them the will to take action. However, experience from inspiration labs shows that sustained influence needs to be linked to paths of learning created that lead to currencies of inspiration. The more human influence, the more human will be able to build sustained communication.

Figure (2) Illustrates the Concept of Inspiration Lab and its Influence

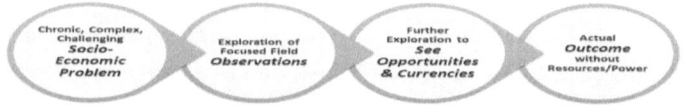

Influence is about exchanging something another person values. It depends a lot on perception and expectations as well as the spirit. Using the spirit of attempting to 'influence without power' in inspiration labs found to create pull thinking that make the participants identify and then extract opportunities and benefits that create positive change with minimal resources. Through executing the radical changes that inspiration labs usually produce, researchers show that influence does not require formal authority or power; however, it does require trust and good relationships at different stages in the lab which supports the work of (Buheji and Thomas, 2016; Vora, 2013).

Through the reflection of inspiration labs experience in the last three years, the power of influence found here to focus on converting the power towards others through empowerment and the utilisation of networks (Buheji and Thomas, 2016).

Since beliefs influence behaviour, inspiration labs focus on creating beliefs through problems findings which create new mindset once problems are solved and became a source of inspiration. Hence, the influence of power is very relevant to the opportunity of finding rather than the capability of solving problems only.

In order to create a sustained inspiration lab, influence human needs to improve the level of visualisation which would improve the accuracy of hit rate. Both visualisation and better hit rate would enhance the direction focus and create a selective mindset that helps to discover and create new learning, as shown in Figure (3). Once the inspiration lab starts to create the outcome human can realise its differentiation in relevance to its ability to create better capacity vs demand (Buheji and Ahmed, 2017).

Figure (3) Constructs of Inspiration Lab influence

Mohamed Buheji & Dunya Ahmed

The currency of 'Influencing without Power' in Inspiration Labs

Currency means something valuable that possess and can trade for something wanted or needed. Currency is valid if human has something to offer others want. So, having a strong currency means that human can create influence with it or even drive change through utilising it effectively. Examples of currencies other than money are having specific technical expertise, specific organisational knowledge, political will, or knowledge about clients, etc. Gratitude, recognition, appreciation, listening, respect, assistance with tasks, are also considered small currencies. Grants and budget allocation are also considered as types of currency.

The currency of 'IWP' generated in inspiration labs helps to change the mindsets of people by selected repetition that affects the logical mind and, at the same time, embraces analogical thinking. This type of currency is enhanced by both failure and an appreciation that creates empathetic thinking. Once this cycle is completed, personal IC becomes even stronger and more focused allowing the creation of positive change in the socio-economy (Buheji and Ahmed, 2017).

Cialdini (2000) talked about using emotional intelligence and empathetic thinking as currencies of 'IWP', giving examples on shopping store staff being cheerful, or when they offer free sampling to taste. This type of influence is part of the art of persuasion.

Currencies of influencing without authority are more effective when there is no direct benefit for the stakeholder you need the help from and is based on 'trading favours' within your network of influence and as a consequence increasing the power of this network.

Finding the right IC is easy, but it need focus on setting the right question. The currency of inspiration comes through the main practice of IE that is observation. With observation, inspiration opportunities can be founded, which once open up to be the right match of what is passionate about it becomes our currency that it is going to use again and again to create an influence.

When the target is to inspire and influence people, organisation and society; raising the capacity to shape what happens next and its effect on the actions, behaviour or opinions of others. Here the IC is about having the focus and curiosity to explore what is happening Buheji and Thomas (2016).

Importance of IC as being a source for raising the capacity to influence through learning generation. Leo van Lier (1996) focused on the importance of the learning generation and mentioned the importance of noticing things in order to learn from them effectively. Once human notice things or ideas then they enter an awareness stage and accept their existence. More noticing means more influence, and more learning. This mean once we enter the stage of realisation, we can 'translate concepts into reality' and this differentiates the level of influence that can be achieved with any socio-economic outcome.

Case Study

Introduction to the Regional Hospital

One of the major regional hospitals in the Gulf Cooperation Council (GCC) was explored to see how its longtime chronic scarcity of emergency beds can be tackled without extra resources and authority. The project targeted to inspire the organisation to improve its total *lead time for emergency beds* and ease admissions in the hospital. The case focused on understanding the basis and the *level of urgency of the cases,* which is one of the most challenging issues in any healthcare institution, especially if this is to be accomplished with no extra resources: *i.e. minimising waiting times without extra resources of beds or staff.* The case study has gone through the following stages to create an effective change through influencing without the need for power:

Understanding the Challenges and Opportunities in the Regional Hospital

This GCC regional hospital had the following challenges that can be turned to opportunities as per IE.

- Despite the hospital had many expansions in the last decade, and it reached a capacity of more than 1600 beds. Still the hospital failed to provide the necessary beds for emergency patients on time.
- There was no proper basis for the data relevant to the availability and management of beds, beds quality services and therefore there was no real-time data that help for beds vacancy management.
- Emergency Patients wait on average more than 12 hours and sometime they might reach 72 hours till they can be admitted as an emergency case.
- The continuous improvement of emergency services and expansion of Accident and Emergency Department, called here for short AandE, needed to accommodate patients waiting for beds inside hospital wards is available.
- There was no consistency of peer reviews and patient satisfaction programmes in relevance to emergency beds turnover.
- The level of the culture of hospitality services in the hospital, in general, was very low.

- The main service provider for emergency cases is the Medical Departments where they have one-fourth of the total hospital bed capacity and get more than one-third of the emergency admitted patients.

Studying how to Motivate and Inspire Residential Physicians with Minimal Power and Without Extra Resources

The following motivation was done in order to excite some of the stakeholders of the emergency bed cases service providers:

- The Medical Department was approached to be the focus of this case study, with the promise of minimal time and efforts would be given from the senior staff to the case study process and not to lose the focus on the core of the service, that is patients quality care.
- The case study facilitator explained to the Medical Department resident physicians why they were chosen instead of consultants to be main partners and team for this management of this project. The Medical residents were mostly young below 30 years old and mostly connected to patients on day and night, besides they are the ones mostly available near patients and usually have better communication abilities with all types of staff, with more patience to manage change.
- After an in-depth dialogue about the importance of the project to their organizational abilities to manage change, the resident physicians were motivated to create a team to carry out data collection, data analysis and auditing.

Mohamed Buheji & Dunya Ahmed

Defining the Type of Inspiration Lab Project

This organisation was selected to be the case study to test the proposed model based on its complexity. This organisation is unique due to its being very resource dependent, managed by professional bureaucrats as medical consultants and senior nurses. The organisation also is very important since it is relevant to critical life services, with multi-discipline staff and with very costly services. Therefore, this inspiration lab was selected to measure how *'influence without power' while defining the inputs and outputs of the project accurately as follows*:

- This hospital is unique as only 16% of the world hospitals have more than 500 beds.
- The hospital accepts many patients who are 65 years old and above who represent the majority of inpatients, even though they are the minority group in our community.
- Even though the majority of patients in these general hospitals would be admitted to a medical department, there is no information for patients' admission and discharge.
- The amount of complaints in this hospital, especially about the quality of treatment in AandE and waiting for admission in medical department is alarming.
- No proper communication plan between departments that would help to ease the complexity of the hospital issue in relevant to being more prepared for emergency cases.

Setting the Scale of Observation for the Project

The following observations were collected to see the sources of influences in the hospital:
- The hospital has 'vertical thinking' (every physician and every department have their own system for patients' discharge).

- The hospital has 'horizontal thinking' between departments to collaborate in order to create better QoL for admitted patients.
- The hospital has 'integrated thinking' that depends on reporting between multidisciplinary teams.

Exploring Inspiration Opportunities

Since many demands are coming up in the healthcare industry that can be either met by more power, supply or building up of better capacity, the inspiration lab helped to explore the following opportunities:

- An opportunity to speed up the availability of beds that leads to lower waiting times to receive emergency service.
- An opportunity to build a model for bed turnover focusing on available improvement techniques to raise the capacity by more 220 beds to accept more patients per week. This would exceptionally viable for meeting a country demand with limited resources.
- An opportunity for increasing the level of medical and health care services provided to patients, since the average age of citizens has increased and there is greater awareness of patients' rights.
- An opportunity for enhancing the level of services must meet hospital accreditation requirements.

This means with these opportunities human can increase the capacity to meet all of these demands without extra resources and without authority: i.e. without changing roles and regulations, or losing the level of patients' confidence in the services.

Mohamed Buheji & Dunya Ahmed

Developing the Way human Think

In order to create the currency of *'influence without power'* in the regional hospital, human need to influence the way people think and act, thus human need to:
- Start collective teams' observations of the work style of medical wards.
- Collectively realise the different patients' treatments are planned.
- Collectively understand the way resident physicians' time is being managed.
- Collectively realise the methods of communication between the wards and other service departments, such as pharmacy, labs, admin. and the bed scheduling team.
- Collectively assess how emergency patients need fast services to be available near the beds they need, in order to speed up the freeing of beds by recovering patients, thus increasing the number of available beds.
- Build team spirit to create better integration of departments through dashboard monitoring of bed turnover per physician.
- Specify which resident physicians prepare the patient release documents.
- Study common disorders that cause patients' demand for beds in the model department which is, in this case, the medical department. This can be supported by creating more explicit protocols and care regarding discharge planning and home follow-ups.

Applying Behavioural Economics

'TWP' *is about Behavioural Economics (BE). In order for BE to occur need to*:

- Enhance the readiness of culture by changing the measures of delay for discharge or bed occupancy from days to hours.
- Establish online synchronisation between medical wards and AandE.
- Set up realisation about the importance of pre-discharge plans.
- Since 78% of patients come from AandE and the discharge time takes more than 10 hours, which need to speed up patients' discharge.
- Most patients stay after 5 pm and even over weekends because no discharge plans have been issued by consultants.
- About 40% of patients in AandE are transferred to medical wards. However, they sometimes need to wait for more than 6 hours; this might be up to 3 days.
- There are high bed occupancy ratios and slow bed turnover.
- Poor facility utilisation and efficiency.

Continuously Reframing the Mindset

Since the ultimate goal of inspiration lab is to create a currency of 'IWP' by changing the mindset of hospital targeted community, this could be realised by working on:
- Values transparency, through maintaining more fairness and empathy.
- Need to have beds for the neediest emergency cases.
- The availability of beds for these cases needs to increase.
- Reduce waiting times for arrival and discharge days.
- There is much instability in the utilisation of beds and turnover in all the wards of medical debts.

Shifting Measures from Outputs to Outcomes

The inspiration Lab techniques mentioned in this case managed to show influence role in transforming the measures from being output (results driven), i.e. to have a bed available however after more than 16 hours, towards being more outcome driven, i.e. the availability of beds guaranteed for emergency patients and especially in Medical Department.

The main root towards 'IWP' currency, in this case, helped to speed up the availability of emergency beds through:
a) Restoring the most optimised measures for admission and discharge that would balance between patients' rights that usually have the Quality-Cost-Delivery build on it.
b) Setting up a pre-discharge communication plan with patients' relatives.
c) Setting up pre-discharge drugs' delivery.
d) I am utilising Total People Involvement (TPI) with both patients and families in the discharge decision.
e) Provision of pharmacy, labs and transport services.

Discussion and Conclusion

A detailed case study has been discussed in relevance to the proposed model of 'IWP' in inspiration labs. The case study shows an innovative approach through different techniques which organisations and communities can use to create great influence with minimal resources and less authority. The other uniqueness of the case is that the conducted influence even more sustainable compared to conventional influence. In this work, the currencies of 'influence without power' model found to develop more opportunities for organisations and communities to get their IE outcome.

Further influence tools as improving the hospital cleanliness and management of the beds to the highest level of patients' satisfaction and reducing the bed costs are not included in this case study reporting. However, many outcomes can be seen as 'IWP' currencies for this case specifically which helped to 60% improvement in emergency patients beds availability, such as the development of discharge checklist. As a result, 90% of the discharge time reduced to before noon daily. This helped to influence the reduction of the average waiting time for the bed to be 1.5 hours.

Other 'influence without power' currencies were pulled along with these outcomes as improving the QoL of patients during bed occupancy and reduction of average waiting time from more than 79 hours to less than 10 hours. A bed management business model was built and proposed that it is more independent of resources and less cost driven.

The case study showed that 'IWP' in inspiration labs create even more peer to peer support while increasing the 'hit rate' by having more intelligent planning achievements. This inspiration influence creates a unique currency of competitiveness that is reflected in the accuracy of forecasting the time of discharge to be raised from 40% to 95% and by the hour. The survey by the type of patient delay during discharge showed very good satisfaction with the services delivered, which are encouraging more change with minimal resources.

Besides showing how inspiration labs influence projects, this case created an improvement in all the related medical protocols, besides elderly care services without the dedication of more resources or more authority. The case also affected the development of admissions and discharges, occupancy rate knowledge management system, and anti-biotic planning. Due to the influence of the case, the hospital decided to start e-consulting with senior consultants and residents in relevant to the patient discharge plan to enhance the management of patient admissions and discharges.

The uniqueness of the case is that it triggered more engagement of hospital decision makers to set up new culture training relevant to patient management for medical residents and interns. A new target was set to reduce bed occupancy by 30% for the most common disorders that occupy patients' beds. This helped to reduce patients' mortality in medical departments specifically by 20%. The final results show that implementation of the bed savings reached about US $20 million, besides reducing patients' suffering.

Despite the limitations of the study being in one country and without being compared to other similar cases, this study has shown that future research about 'IWP' currency in similar areas is highly encouraged to reduce the capital economy resource dependency syndrome. In comparison to almost all the work on 'influencing without authority' this work opens a new direction on the concept of influence and how it can create a major differentiation on the socio-economic development and stability, (Cialdini, 2000; Larson, 2006; Stakeholder Management, 2016; Yukl, and Falbe, 1990; Porter et al, 2015; Yukl and Falbe, 1990;, Trzcielinski, 2013; Tescula and Ruckm, 2000; Westwood, F (2001) Westwood, 2001; Leo, 1996). Such studies would help to change not only individuals mindsets, but even countries strategies.

References

Buheji, M and Ahmed, D (2017) Breaking the Shield: Introduction to Inspiration Engineering: Philosophy, Practices and Success Stories, Archway Publishing, USA.

Buheji, M and Thomas, B (2016) Handbook of Inspiration Economy, Bookboon.

Cialdini, R (1984) Influence - The Psychology of Persuasion, HarperCollins

Cialdini, R (2000) Influence: Science and Practice: United States Edition, Pearson; 4th edition

Cohen, A., and Bradford, D. (2005). Influence Without Authority (2nd ed.). New Jersey: Wiley.

Gottwald, W. D. (2008). Influence without authority and navigating through internal politics. Paper presented at PMI® Global Congress 2008—North America, Denver, CO. Newtown Square, PA: Project Management Institute. https://www.pmi.org/learning/library/influence-without-authority-six-step-process-7018, accessed: 2/1/2018

Hill, Linda (1994) Exercising Influence, Harvard Business School, Case Studies Collection and Background Note 494-080, February. https://www.hbs.edu/faculty/Pages/item.aspx?num=16525, accessed: 12/12/2017

Hogg, M and Cooper, J (2007) The SAGE Handbook of Social Psychology: Concise Student Edition

Johnson, L (2008) Exerting Influence Without Authority, Feb 28, Harvard Business Review, https://hbr.org/2008/02/exerting-influence-without-aut, accessed: 2/1/2018

Kendrick, T (2012) Results Without Authority: Controlling a Project When the Team Does not Report to You, 2nd Edition, American Management Association.

Larson, E. and Larson, R. (2006). Influencing without authority: rev up your internal consulting skills. Paper presented at PMI Global Congress 2006—North America, Seattle, WA. Newtown Square, PA: Project Management Institute. https://www.pmi.org/learning/library/influencing-without-authority-project-requirements-8100, accessed: 2/1/2018

Leo van Lier (1996) Interaction in the language curriculum: Awareness, Autonomy and Authenticity (Applied Linguistics and Language Study Series). London: Longman.

Mathieu, J. E., Heffner, T. S., Goodwin, G. F., Salas, E., and Cannon-Bowers, J. A. (2000) The influence of shared mental models on team process and performance. Journal of Applied Psychology, 85, 273–283

Porter, L; Angle, H and Allen, R (2015) Organizational Influence Processes, second edition, Routledge.

Probst, J (2017) Influence Without Authority Whitepaper Principal Consultant Pink Elephant http://www1.pinkelephant.com/PinkLINK/na/issue192/Influence-Without-Authority.pdf, accessed: 2/1/2018

Stakeholder Management (2016) Influence without authority, Project Knowledge Index, https://mosaicprojects.com.au/Mag_Articles/SA1025_Influence_without_authority.pdf, accessed: 2/1/2018

Tescula, T and Ruckm, C (2000) Influencing Without Authority, Chicago Annual Meeting, Society of Actuaries, October 15–18.

Trzcielinski, S (2013) The Influence of Knowledge-Based Economy on Agility of Enterprise, 6th International Conference on Applied Human Factors and Ergonomics (AHFE 2015) and the Affiliated Conferences, AHFE 2015, Procedia Manufacturing 3, pp. 6615 – 6623.

Vora, T (2013) 6 Lessons On Creating a Lasting Influence, Insights, Resources and Visual Notes on Leadership, Learning and Change, http://qaspire.com/2013/09/22/6-lessons-on-creating-a-lasting-influence/, Accessed: 11/11/2017

Westwood, F (2001) Influencing Without Power, British Journal of Pre-Operative Nursing, Vol 1, No.11, pp. 499–502, Nov.

Yukl, G. and Falbe, M. (1990). Influence tactics and objectives in upward, downward, and lateral influence attempts. *Journal of Applied Psychology, 75*(2), 132-140. http://dx.doi.org/10.1037/0021-9010.75.2.132, accessed: 2/1/2018

Yukl, G., and Falbe, C. M. (1990). Influence tactics and objectives in upward, downward, and lateral influence attempts. *Journal of Applied Psychology, 75*(2), 132-140. http://dx.doi.org/10.1037/0021-9010.75.2.132

CHAPTER 6

Influence of Visualised Reflection on "Solving Socio-Economic Problems"- A Case from Youth Economy Forums[6]

Introduction

Reflection is a very important process that creates meanings in our life journey, especially after careful thought about our behaviour, experiences and beliefs, (Shorrab, 2016). Reflection as per Shorrab can be about the self, or the surroundings; or nature, or own experiences, or even about others experiences.

In this chapter, we will discuss the importance of Critical Reflection and Reflective Thinking, after defining each of them. Then reflection through learning and meaning journey is reviewed, followed by the psychologic and cognitive processs of reflection. The influence of reflection on solving socio-economic problems is studied after understanding how reflection perform based on intention and visualisation. The relation of youth

---

[6] Buheji, M (2019) Influence of visualised reflection on 'solving socio-economic problems' – a case from youth economy forums, **Int. J. Innovation and Learning**, 25 (1), pp. 1-16.

economy and reflection management. Critical reflection and influence of reflection from the socio-economic perspective is reviewed in detail.

The methodological approach used in this chapter help to study the influence of youth economy reflection practices during the projects carried out by the youth teams before, during and after the forum of youth economy in Bosnia and Herzegovina. Teams observations and their participation in feedback surveys helped to come with the results and conclusions presented in this study.

This research questions whether youth capacity for solving socio-economic problems can be enhanced through specific procedures that would enhance their visualisation and critical reflection. Therefore, the criterion for the evaluation of project teams outcomes and innovativeness is set.

The significance of such study is that it would enhance the youth capacity to creating positive change in their societies in the process of learning and social innovation efforts. Also, such study illustrates the importance of youth integration with socio-economic projects.

Definition of Reflection

Webster's International Dictionary considers reflection as a "mental consideration of some subject matter, idea or purpose, often with a view to understanding or accepting it, or seeing it in its right relations". Webster also defines reflection as a calm, lengthy intent consideration.

What is involved in reflection? "Reflection is part of learning and thinking. We reflect on learning something, or we learn as a result of reflecting, and the term 'reflective learning' emphasises the intention to learn from current or prior experience" (Moon 2004). Reflection as per Shorrab (2016) is more of a process of internally examining and exploring an issue of concern, triggered by an experience, which creates and clarifies meaning regarding self, and which results in a changed conceptual perspective, it is a process requires the attitude that value emotions. This process helps to make 'meaning' and a sense of experience, after interpreting it. When we subsequently use this interpretation to guide decision-making or action, then making 'meaning' becomes 'learning'.

Therefore, one can summarise that reflection is a type of thinking aimed at achieving better understanding and leading to new learning. All of the following are important aspects of the reflective process, which reflect in summary the "drive of making sense of experience".

Critical Reflection

Critical reflection often happens as a result of the dynamic interaction between habit and the event being interpreted. The process is often mediated by reflection. Critical reflection is significantly involved when we look back on content or procedural assumptions guiding the problem-solving process to reassess the efficacy of the strategies and tactics used.

Mezirow (1998) was one of the earliest who clarified the major role of critical reflection due to assumptions (CRA) and how it affects youth and adult learning. Mezirow seen critical reflection can be intentionally practised and developed over the lifespan. CRA as per Mezirow research is very relevant to the validation of beliefs and expressions of feelings, since it involves assessment of assumption that constructs the belief. Therefore, Mezirow and other researchers saw that CRA can increase even our beliefs about how to solve problems. Brookfield, (1987).

Researchers become critically reflective by challenging the established definition of a problem being addressed, perhaps by finding a new metaphor that reorients problem-solving efforts more effectively. By far the most significant learning experience involve critical self-reflection, i.e. through reassessing the way we have posed problems and reassessing our orientation to perceiving, knowing, believing, feeling and acting. Critical reflection is not concerned with how or the how-to of action, but with the why, the reasons for and the consequences of what we do. Gay and Kirkland (2010).

While meaning schemes and perspectives are built through basic reflection. More in-depth meaning perspectives, which determine what, how, and why we learn, cannot be absorbed without critical reflection.

Reynolds (1998) shown contrasts of the concept of critical reflection drawing on the work of critical theorists in adult education-with the more familiar concept of 'reflection'. Reynolds proposed how the principles of critical reflection might be applied to management education practice; the distinction is made between educational content (the curriculum) and educational process (methods and structures), drawing attention to the need to consider both in the development of a 'critical' management pedagogy.

Cope (2003) studied the importance of 'learning events' which has become a new theme within theorising on how entrepreneurs learn. It has been argued that there is more to learning from discontinuous events than the incremental accumulation of more routinised, habitual, 'lower-level' learning. These events have the capacity to stimulate distinctive forms of 'higher-level' learning—learning that is fundamental to the entrepreneur.

What is Reflective Thinking and Why it is Important?

Reflective thinking is different from critical thinking. Critical thinking is about using cognitive skills or strategies that increase the probability of a desirable outcome, i.e. thinking that is purposeful, reasoned and goal-directed. It is a kind of thinking involved in solving problems, formulating inferences and calculating likelihoods. Therefore, critical thinking is sometimes called directed thinking because it focuses on the desired outcome. Halpern (1996).

Reflective thinking focuses on shifting individuals' capability from making decisions based on opinions to making judgments, as seen by King and Kitchener (1993). However, reflective thinking is most important in promoting learning during complex problem-solving situations because it provides an opportunity to step back and think about how problems are solved. Teekman (2000).

Dewey (1938) seen that reflective thinking importance comes from its role in creating an active and persistent belief. Reflective learning helps people to assess what they know, what they need to know, and how they bridge that gap during learning situations.

The reflective thinking demands attention to both terms "reflection" and "thinking" especially in problem-based learning. During this journey of individuals would seek ground learning in a more authentic environment that exists in the traditional classrooms.

Modern society is becoming more complex; information is becoming available and changing more rapidly prompting users to rethink, switch directions, and change problem-solving strategies constantly. Thus, it is increasingly important to prompt reflective thinking during learning to help learners develop strategies to apply new knowledge to the complex situations in their day-to-day activities. King and Kitchener (1993) and Buheji (2017a).

Reflection through Learning and Meaning Journey

Erlendsson (2001) found that it is not possible to understand the nature of youth and adult learning, or education without taking into account the role of habits to make and build the meaning. Meaning schemes are sets in structures of related and habitual expectations as 'if-then', or 'cause-effect'; such relations help to categorise relationships as well as event sequences.

Meaning build perspectives through first setting assumption, theories, propositions, beliefs, prototypes and goal orientations. Through meaning, we build the capacity for evaluation which is assimilated depending on the level of experience to lead to a broad interpretation. Erlendsson (2001). Meaning perspectives help to establish reflective judgement, as the exercise of meaning involves criteria for making 'value judgements' and for our reference belief in our systems, King and Kitchener (1993).

Reflection should always be differentiated from thinking or learning, since reflection is part of them and it helps to assess the grounds (justification) of one's beliefs. If utilised and controlled the effect of experience, reflections strengthen, extends, and refines our structures of meaning by reinforcing our expectations about how things are supposed to be. Our habits of expectation are not merely taken-for-granted actions or reactions that tend to repeat themselves. They are dispositions and capabilities that make up our everyday involvement within structures that 'make sense'.

Psychology and Cognitive Process of Reflection

Reflection is generally used as a synonym for higher-order mental processes. Boud et al. (1985) seen reflection as an intellectual and affective activity in which individuals engage to explore their experiences to lead to new understandings and appreciation. There is a cognitive process during reflection that helps us to make enough inferences, look for generalisations, try analogies and do our final evaluations. This cognitive exercise builds psychological feelings, which enhance remembering and curiosity for problem-solving. This, in turn, raises the belief in the capacity for useful interpretation to analyse, to synthesis, perform, discuss and final judge. This judgement, however, is still influenced by the 'habits of expectation' that constitute our 'frame of reference' which helps to build what we perceive and think and hence build our structure of interpretation.

Erlendsson (2001) seen that habits of expectation help even to build personal constructs, perceptual filters, conceptual maps, metaphors, personal ideologies, repressed functions and developmental stages. These habits define then the learning styles and the ethical basis and thus control meanings references which lead to the reflective judgement.

Experience sometimes plays the main obstacle on the way we think or learn, or try to reflect critically. Experience tends to resort to psychological defence mechanisms and disable us to elaborate more. Mainly experience help to reinforce long-established frames of reference to create what is thought to be new meaning schemes. Reflective interpretation is the process of correcting distortions in our reasoning and attitudes which help to over the experience blockage. Once experience blockage is overcome critical reflection would help them to accurately identify the distinguished patterns of similarity and build new metaphoric labels.

Innovativeness of Reflection Process Based on Utilising Intention and Visualisation

After understanding how reflection goes through learning and meaning journey and what is the cognitive psychological framework of it, it is time to ask what differentiate the influence of certain reflections from the others?

Erlendsson (2001) emphasised fostering critical reflection that triggers differentiated transformative learning occurs when we 'learn to perform' rather than when we 'learn to understand'. Therefore, Govaerts et al. (2010) seen that once we start the intention through visualising what the outcome should be, we start the process of searching for defined specific meanings. These meanings lead to building specific awareness that direct the journey for specific type of knowledge collection and starting waves of empathetic thinking about what is absorbed. Therefore, one could say that we build meanings in reality by building our perspectives. Thus through these perspectives, we build than the principles for 'our' interpretations which involve symbol systems that represent 'ideal types', the qualities of which we project onto objects or events in our experience. What we then perceive is often seen as an instance of our symbolic categories.

Visualisation is highly related to the capacity for achieving the meaning planned as with visualisation the habits of expectation structure is created, then the meaning in the brain create storage of bins in the memory. Love (1995). The chess players see one of the best examples of the importance of visualization. The players usually take a time of thoughtful action, i.e. visualising the outcome of the move before actually being actively engaged. Therefore, through visualisation reflection become an action that is predicated on a critical assessment of assumptions, may also be an integral part of decision making.

Influence of Reflection on Innovativeness in Solving Socio-Economic Problems

Shorrab (2016) seen that with reflection we can establish more innovation cycles which can start with reflection, followed by inspiration and the eager to do more experimentation that would lead to certainty. Reflection enables us to correct distortions in our beliefs and errors in problem-solving.

In everyday situations, we challenge the validity of what is being communicated when we have doubts about the truth, comprehensibility, appropriateness or authenticity. Thoughtful action is reflexive but is not the same thing as acting reflectively to examine the justification for one's beliefs critically. The pause that happens after visualisation help to optimise the decision-making process. Here reflection would be an integral part of performing and an element of thoughtful action. Kolb (1984).

Manski (1993) mentioned about how the reflection problem arises when a researcher observing the distribution of behaviour in a population tries to infer whether the average behaviour in some group influences the behaviour of the individuals that comprise the group. It has been found that inference is not possible unless the researcher has prior information specifying the composition of reference groups. If this information is available, the prospects for inference depend critically on the population relationship between the variables defining reference groups and those directly affecting outcomes.

Smyth (1989) provided background information on the emergence of reflectivity as a conceptual thrust. Smyth concludes to uncover the forces that inhibit and constrain them; they need to be engaged in four forms of action. These "forms" are characterized by four sequential stages and are linked to a series of questions: (a) describing (What do we need to do?), (b) informing (What does this mean?), (c) confronting (How did I come to be like this?), and (d) reconstructing (How might I do things differently?). These sequences help to raise the innovativeness in solving any complex problem. Therefore, reflection during socio-economic driven projects can serve as a philosophical foundation and as criteria for judging the social conditions prerequisite and reflective discourse that would help the final interpretation. Moulaert and Nussbaumer (2005).

Mohamed Buheji & Dunya Ahmed

Youth Economy and Reflection Management

The importance of reflecting on improving the socio-economy as part of the learning process has been emphasised by Moulaert and Nussbaumer (2005). Grabher (1993) suggested that the capacity to reflect on action to engage in the process of continuous learning is very important for the development of a differentiated professional mindset.

Lee-Kelley and Blackman (2005) shown the importance of a receptive environment to the continuous challenge of teams for creating an effective, innovative mindset that provides flexible solutions. The conclusion of Lee-Kelley and Blackman study shown that teams would deliver better outcomes if they can establish new ideas through the development of their knowledge. In this chapter, the knowledge development is zoomed to be the outcome of the visualised reflection.

Schön (1983) describes the reflective practice as a professional activity in which the practitioner reflects, both in-action and on-action to improve his or her practice. Reflection can result in deeper society learning and innovative development if embedded in youth assumptions, beliefs, and values are challenged. The earlier work of Buheji (2017b) shows that youth economy project should be based on transformative learning which involves a particular function of reflection. This means that the projects should help to reassess the presuppositions on which youth beliefs are based and act on developing a transformed meaning perspective as a result of projects re-assessments.

Methods

Introduction to the Methodological Approach

The methodological approach here below is described more in details and set the process of how the data was gathered. The methodology of this study target to help see the influence of youth economy practices during the forums of youth economy specifically carried in Bosnia and Herzegovina. The methodology of a qualitative approach to see the reactions of the projects teams. Teams observations and feedback surveys are carried out throughout the period of the study.

Teams were divided according to the main issues and problems that were observed during the researchers' earlier field visit. Each youth team had a clear mandate and objectives for the expected outcomes. In addition, they all had at least one institution that they worked with and where they applied their prototype. Moreover, a full week workshop was conducted for one week, to make sure that that all team members had a good understanding of their roles and what was expected of them.

The young people participated in the project voluntarily after it was announced in local media and social media with the support of academics in Bihac University, Colleges and schools.

Introduction of the Project to the Team Members

A collection of twenty-five youth students of ages between 15 till 22 years were distributed equally on five teams. Each of the five teams had a university professor as a mentor. All the teams were from Bosnia and Herzegovina and focused on creating a model that shows the influence of youth in tackling five different socio-economic issues related to youth. The first issue was 'youth quality of life and poverty'. The second issue was tackled by the 'youth values and gambling (betting)' team. The third youth team was dedicated to 'voluntary youth contribution through civic organisations'. The fourth team was about youth 'entrepreneurship and innovation' programs. The fifth and last team was the youth 'migration mitigation' team.

The teams were given three workshops; the first one was to understand their roles and build team spirit and cohesion, besides defining clearly the team scope. The second workshop targeted to incorporate visualisation of the socio-economic outcome of each team and the role of youth economy currency, if clear target is set through clear intention and belief of capacity to deal with problems, without or with minimal, resources and authority.

Team Exercise on Visualisation and Critical Reflection

An exercise on visualisation and reflective thinking were carried by the researcher, using music and drawings of a butterfly with and without music to show the importance of visualisation for effective critical reflection.

Each team was given months of June till early September to frequently meet, collect the data and do early reflections with the researcher on the socio-economic model and outcome visualised, every two weeks. Each team was asked to follow the template slides to get a focused reflection from all the stakeholders of the project, including the teams' members, the beneficiaries, the mentors, the invited evaluating experts and youth forum participants.

The templates for Stage 1 (i.e. before the forum) and Stage 2 (after the forum) were similar. The purpose was to compare the difference in visualisation and critical reflections of each of the youth teams and see how this visualisation influenced their socio-economic outcome and model innovativeness.

Criteria for the Evaluation of Each Team Project Outcome and Innovativeness

Youth Project Stage 1 & Stage 2 Template Slides were distributed to each of the teams with the purpose to show the model innovativeness. Each template included the following:
a) Guidance on the youth economy project criteria's where each Criteria worth 10 points. It also included what visualisation and reflection should be included in each project presentation.
b) The criterions were as follows:
    1. Commitment to exploring the visualised socio-economic problem and targeted outcome within each project.
    2. Implementation story visualised that would turn the problem to a success story and a model of reference.
    3. Challenges that have been (or would be) overcome with time.
    4. How would the project help in inspiring the community and youth in the targeted community or scope?
    5. How is the project visualised to help trigger inspiration and youth empowerment in different potential projects?
    6. What are the different attempts that send a message about the capacity of youth economy in creating a difference to their socio-economic problems?
    7. *How the project* focus on priorities & of importance to youth problems or related to it?
    8. How is the project driven by evidence-based measurements?
    9. How does the project help to discover the "intrinsic powers" of each youth and team members?
    10. How the project was done based on "minimal resources" and while utilising partnership and "people involvement"?

The youth team members were asked to deliver a clear message by action *"yes we can be an inspiring and value-added youth and make a great difference in our community"*.

Mohamed Buheji & Dunya Ahmed

Direction for Teams to enhance the Outcome Innovativeness

In order to enhance the practice of visualisation and reflection, each team was asked to simply observe and then discuss and identify collectively together with the socio-economic problem the team want to tackle and visualise the opportunities for solutions, through doing (not talking). i.e. to include a visualisation of how the projects would lead to better socio-economy. Each team was asked to prepare too for questions from the forum visiting experts on why the team is chosen or visualised this focused area of the project scope, based on the observations collected and refined.

More expectation about reflection recommendation was deployed to each team during the researcher one to one teams' meetings that were carried during June till early September. The teams were asked to specify only one or two small areas of the socio-economic problem that they recommend to tackle next innovatively and what type of areas need to be investigated. This reflection should include evidence from the data and visits outcomes.

In order to enhance their visualisation besides showing their differentiated innovativeness, all the teams were strictly asked to use tables, graphs and photos in their presentation and during meetings discussions. Also, all teams were frequently reminded to use both measures (i.e. surveys, questionnaires, interviews) and Indicators (that are measured by count and usually published by large entities, incl. the government).

The Evaluation Procedures during the Teams Presentation during the Youth Economy Forum

As early September approached, teams were asked to prepare a focused presentation about the results of the five projects and discuss it together, to see the level of achievement of the visualised outcome and to learn to reflect together on the results before the forum experts have their inputs too on it.

During the Forum of Youth Economy, in middle of September, experts from five different countries were asked on reflecting on the work of each of the five teams and general forum discuss was opened too to enhance the feedback. A collection of data and interview with experts measured to see the status of achievement of each team, the role of visualisation of each the solution proposed as a model of each of the tackled socio-economic problem and how they believed the reflection played a role in the development of youth economy influence on these problems.

The Evaluation of Experts & Mentors

The team mentors and experts were asked during the youth economy forum to discuss how the project goes on using the visualisation and critical reflection tools? What processes or methodologies they both believed can be used to create effective visualisation and critical reflections that influence the outcome of youth on the socio-economy? i.e. was it the workshops, the researcher focused meetings, the visualisation exercise of the butterfly, the criteria's, the teams frequent meetings, the data collections, the use of the use tables, graphs and photos, etc.

The Evaluation of Experts & Forum Participants

The experts and forum participants were asked in September to evaluate whether the visualisation and reflection help the enhance the communication between the team members and their mentors in order to create a solution for the socio-economic problem? In addition, how they seen the critical factors that help the youth to create their success in relevant to the complex issue tackled.

Mohamed Buheji & Dunya Ahmed

Scoring the Overall Evaluation for each Team Influence on the Socio-economic Outcome.

The researcher established a scoring system for that measure the main influence of visualisation and critical reflection. The scores for each variable was set from 1 (very weak) until 5 (very strong). The scores were estimated to nearest possible number, based on the discussion with the main project's stakeholders: teams peer-to-peer evaluation, team mentors, visiting forum experts, forum participants and beneficiaries. All collectively calculated to show how far each team managed to use the visualisation and critical reflection in tackling the socio-economic problem in exploring their youth economy currency. The total scores were to be presented as part of the summary of the results of each team in relevance in relevance to their selected project. The table was set to include the visualisation seen, the critical reflection, the accuracy of visualised outcome and finally the importance of the model for the socio-economic problem tackled.

Each team were asked to explain in detail their model project in relevant to the socio-economic outcome, to be considered as part of the evaluation table.

Results

The youth economy projects and practice of visualisation and then critical reflection brought lots of learning and innovation benefits that created a radical change in the participating youth mindsets, besides raising their aspirations. This three-month exercise helped youth to see the big picture in their role in life, i.e. build more life purposefulness, besides feeling they are empowered.

The main results of this case study were that youth are being able to make a more creative change in their socio-economy without the dependency on major resources or authority. Besides, maturity in proper judgements was noticed based on facts.

Both 'early workshops', showing the importance of visualisation in relevance to critical reflection and 'post workshops' meeting helped the youth team members to start to believe that they can make a differentiated, innovative socio-economic model for their community. To evaluate the innovativeness of achieved socio-economic model proposed and implemented by each of the five teams, the main project's stakeholders: teams peer-to-peer, the team mentors, the visiting forum experts, the forum participants and the beneficiaries have all been asked to do a separate evaluation. Then the results of each team were tabulated after they have been summed. The tabulation in Table (1) meant to show how far each team managed to use the visualisation and critical reflection in tackling the socio-economic problem and exploring their youth economy currency. The different summary of the results of each team selected project in Table (1) is meant to show the specific innovative models created and along with the level of: utilisation of visualisation, critical reflection, the accuracy of visualised outcome and finally the importance of the model for the socio-economy of the community and youth.

Table (1) illustrates each of the Teams Performance Scores in relevance to the influence of visualisation and critical reflection on the Socio-Economic Problem Tackled.

Table 1-a Team Project: Youth Quality of Life and Poverty

Models Innovativeness:
    a) Measuring of type of Youth's Risks on Quality of Life.
    b) Engagement of Youth with Humanitarian Agency to Improve Youth under poverty Quality of Life.

Youth Economy Projects Evaluation	Visualisation	Critical Reflection	Accuracy of Visualised Outcome	Importance of Model for Socio-Economic Problem
Peer-to-Peer Team Evaluation	5	4	3	5
Visiting Experts Evaluation	4	4	4	4
Team Mentors Evaluation	5	5	3	5
Youth Economy Forum Participants Evaluation	4	4	5	5

Table 1-b Team Project: Youth Values and Gambling (Betting)

Models Innovativeness:
    a) Focusing on Youth and Family Values by Two Women Driven NGO's
    b) Fostering a Program for Creating a Betting Free School

Youth Economy Projects Evaluation	Visualisation	Critical Reflection	Accuracy of Visualised Outcome	Importance of Model for Socio-Economic Problem
Peer-to-Peer Team Evaluation	3	4	3	4
Visiting Experts Evaluation	4	4	4	5
Team Mentors Evaluation	3	3	3	4
Youth Economy Forum Participants Evaluation	5	3	5	5

Table 1-c Team Project: Youth Voluntary Contribution through Civic Organisations

Models Innovativeness:
  a) Measuring the contribution of youth in youth-related NGO's and their influence on Youth Aspiration
  b) Measuring and Enhancing the effectiveness of extra-Curricular youth civic engagement programs
  c) Studying Success Stories of Youth Voluntary Models and Successful Youth NGO's
  d) Focusing on building a Strong Youth Engagement in One of the Sports Clubs

Youth Economy Projects Stakeholders Evaluation	Visualisation	Critical Reflection	Accuracy of Visualised Outcome	Importance of Model for Socio-Economic Problem
Peer-to-Peer Team Evaluation	5	4	4	5
Visiting Experts Evaluation	5	4	4	3
Team Mentors Evaluation	5	3	4	4
Youth Economy Forum Participants Evaluation	5	4	4	5

Table 1-d Team Project: Youth Entrepreneurship and Innovation

Models Innovativeness:
  a) Measuring the contribution of youth in youth-related NGO's
  b) Measuring and Enhancing the effectiveness of extra-Curricular youth civic engagement programs
  c) Studying Success Stories of Youth Entrepreneurs in the Country

d) Establishing a Partnership Program with the Chamber of Commerce that is dedicated to the development of Youth Entrepreneurship and Innovation.

Youth Economy Projects Stakeholders Evaluation	Visualisation	Critical Reflection	Accuracy of Visualised Outcome	Importance of Model for Socio-Economic Problem
Peer-to-Peer Team Evaluation	3	3	4	4
Visiting Experts Evaluation	4	3	3	3
Team Mentors Evaluation	3	4	4	4
Youth Economy Forum Participants Evaluation	3	3	3	3

Table 1-e Team Project: Migration Mitigation

Models Innovativeness:
    a) Measuring the extent of the Risks of Youth Migration in relevance to educational and government programs
    b) Measuring and enhancing the effectiveness of extra-Curricular youth programs about the potentials and opportunities of the country
    c) Studying success stories of Migrants who came back or those youths chose to stay in the country
    d) Establishing a partnership program to mitigate the risk of youth migration.

Youth Economy Projects Stakeholders Evaluation	Visualisation	Critical Reflection	Accuracy of Visualised Outcome	Importance of Model for Socio-Economic Problem
Peer-to-Peer Team Evaluation	3	3	2	5
Visiting Experts Evaluation	3	3	3	5
Team Mentors Evaluation	3	3	2	5
Youth Economy Forum Participants Evaluation	3	4	2	5

Discussion

The methodology and results show the importance of the cultivation of the capacity of youth in influencing their socio-economic conditions through the utilisation of visualisation and critical reflection (while doing the projects) and (after doing projects). This methodology of setting youth engagement and involvement through first structured workshops and then unstructured data collection about the specific socio-economic problem and how it is essential for many disciplines and not only in management.

Going back to the literature review, we can see that visualisation help to enhance the effectiveness of the youth pauses taken during the journey of each of the teams' projects. The critical reflection with a visualised outcome relevant to each of the five teams' themes provided a way of 'standing back' from the emotions and better judgments.

The exercise of critical reflection which involves 'going over' specific project visualised outcome, often several times, in order to explore what happened or need to happen from different points of view help to reach the outcome and enhance the youth engagement with the socio-economic project. This created, in turn, the youth economy currency. Critical reflection enables youth to plan their influence with foresight and to plan according to ends-in-view, or to come into command of what is now distant and lacking.

The measurement of the visualisation also found to enhance the balanced youth judgement. The critical reflection found to enhance the team members learning and engagement on the projects that cannot be taught. Overall, the exercise raised the curiosity and the spirit of inquiry for each participant.

The qualitative method for data collections through observations and then followed by feedback showed that major leaps happen when youth visualise the outcome of their holistic thinking. Youth once start the visualisation would consequently start the collection of data and observation with high exploratory, logical and analogical spirit. Besides, youth would build overtime an empathetic, curious mindset that leads to both deductive and inductive thinking.

The projects of youth address the United Nations Millennium Sustainable Development Goals (SDGs) from 2015 – 2030, as they address issues that tackle poverty, besides the promotion of volunteering, knowledge sharing and values development. The process of the holistic youth engagement through the outcomes of their projects visualisation and reflection help to build their self-confidence and critical thinking. The youth projects evaluated in this chapter help to develop youth spirit and lead to social activated participation.

Providing visualisation and reflection helped to align youth activities and build their capacity to draw evidence-based conclusions for complex socio-economic problems and challenges. Reflective thinking help to provide youth opportunities to choose and implement the best alternatives and thus to realise more their intrinsic power.

The impact of these results in that even though most of the study was developed based a practical methodology for delivery of a youth-driven project, the stream of the flow between youth mindset and both the visualisation and critical reflection can lead to important socio-economic models and results.

Conclusion

The methodology of measuring the influence of visualised reflection is based on an action based research which involved a group youth who were the medium for the data collected and who were involved in projects that validated the data. The young teams collected and analysed the data themselves. However, the strength of the research results is that each team implemented their project in a different setting and met different challenges. All the team were evaluated according to the outputs of their handling of the socio-economic problem tackled and then on the level of their visualised reflection.

The key findings from the study help improve the learning and development of youth once they are involved earlier with the project visualisation and then reflect on their project outcome in relevance to that visualisation. The combination of carefully designed youth visualisation and critical reflection provide the possibility to identify and clarify overall socio-economic problems. Both visualisation and critical reflection provide different opportunities to show the influence of youth and youth economy on solving or dealing with socio-economic issues, as complex as poverty and migration as we have seen in the case study discussed. The amount of youth capacity to have highly focused outcomes found it can be highly enhanced through having possible causes and solutions, i.e. visualisation and critical reflection.

Since youth were always seen as being slow in learning from their experiences, they need projects that enhance their visualisation, sharpen their reflection, so that they can 'make sense' and analyse their experience while actively make meaning of it. Visualisation and critical reflection can be particularly useful in a youth-driven economy to deal with difficult or challenging socio-economic situations. The intention to solve socio-economic problems help youth to incorporated a better learning capacity in their life journey.

The presentation of different models for each of the socio-economic problem showed that raising the innovativeness of youth influence and engagement need not to be always seen as a complex issue, regardless of the complexity of the problem. The final impact of this study is that it supports the research on the cycle of learning that leads to shifting in mindset and real youth empowerment, be it through workshops, forum, extra-curricular classes, etc. The chapter emphasis that learning and innovativeness of youth can be enhanced by visualising and reviewing the outcome expected by simple system and structures. The researcher highly recommends that such study be followed by more longitudinal studies to optimise the utilisation of youth visualised reflection in solving further socio-economic problems in different countries, thus overcoming the study geographical limitation.

Reference

Brookfield, S (1998). Critically reflective practice, *Journal of Continuing Education in the Health Professions* 18 (4): 197–205.

Brookfield, S. (1987). Developing critical thinkers. San Francisco; Jossey-Bass.

Buheji, M (2017a) Understanding Problem-Solving in Inspiration Labs, American Journal of Industrial and Business Management, 7, pp. 771-784, http://file.scirp.org/pdf/AJIBM_2017062216580094.pdf

Buheji, M (2017b) In Search of the Inspired Student—Measuring of Youth Inspiration in High School—A Youth Economy-Paper American Journal of Industrial and Business Management, 7, pp. 785-797, http://file.scirp.org/pdf/AJIBM_2017062217064036.pdf

Boud, D., Keogh, R. & Walker, D. (1985) Reflection: Turning Experience into Learning. London: Kogan Page.

Cope, J (2003) Entrepreneurial Learning and Critical Reflection, Discontinuous Events as Triggers for 'Higher-level' Learning, Management Learning, Volume: 34 issue: 4, page(s): 429-450, December 1.
https://doi.org/10.1177/1350507603039067

Dewey, J. (1938) Logic: The Theory of Inquiry. MN: Rinehart & Winston

Edutopia (2011) – Reflections Questions, 21st-century Learning Academy
https://www.edutopia.org/pdfs/stw/edutopia-stw-replicatingPBL-21stCAcad-reflection-questions.pdf

Erlendsson, J (2001) Reflective Thinking, Educational Productivity. **https://notendur.hi.is/joner/eaps/wh_refl7.htm**, Accessed:19/1/2018

Gay, G and Kirkland, K (2010) Developing Cultural Critical Consciousness and Self-Reflection in Preservice Teacher Education, Journal of Theory Into Practice, Volume 42, - Issue 3, Pages 181-187, Published online: 24 Jun,

Govaerts, S; Verbert, K; Klerkx, J and Duval, E (2010) Visualizing Activities for Self-reflection and Awareness,
https://lirias.kuleuven.be/bitstream/123456789/283362/1/icwlSten.pdf
Accessed: 1/1/2018

Halpern, D. F. (1996). Thought and knowledge: an introduction to critical thinking (3rd ed.). Mahwah, NJ: L. Erlbaum Associates.

Hatton, N and Smith, D (1995) Reflection in teacher education: Towards definition and implementation. Teaching and Teacher Education. Vol 11, Issue 1, pp. 33-49

Hedberg, P (2008) Learning Through Reflective Classroom Practice, Applications to Educate Reflective Manager, Journal of Management Education Vol 33, Issue 1

King, P. and Kitchener K. (1993). Developing reflective judgment. San Francisco: Jossey-Bass

Lee-Kelley L and Blackman D, (2005) In addition to shared goals: The impact of mental models on team innovation and learning, International Journal of Innovation and Learning, vol. 2, pp. 11-25.

Lin, X., Hmelo, C., Kinzer, C. K., & Secules, T. J (1999). Designing technology to support reflection, Educational Technology Research & Development, pp. 43-62.

Love E. (1995) The Functions of Visualisation in Learning Geometry. In: Sutherland R., Mason J. (eds) Exploiting Mental Imagery with Computers in Mathematics Education. NATO ASI Series (Series F: Computer and Systems Sciences), vol 138. Springer, Berlin, Heidelberg

Manski, C (1993) Identification of Endogenous Social Effects: The Reflection Problem. The Review of Economic Studies, Volume 60, Issue 3, 1 July 1993, Pages 531–542, https://doi.org/10.2307/2298123

Mezirow, J (1998) On Critical Reflection, Adult Education Quarterly, Volume: 48 issue: 3, page(s): 185-198, Issue published: May 1, https://doi.org/10.1177/074171369804800305

Moon, J. A. (1999). Reflection in learning and professional development: Theory and practice. London: Kogan Page.

Moulaert, F and Nussbaumer (2005) Defining the Social Economy and its Governance at the Neighbourhood Level:

A Methodological Reflection, Volume: 42 issue: 11, page(s): 2071-2088 https://doi.org/10.1080/420980500279752

Reflective thinking, John Dewey and PBL, http://www.imsa.edu/~bernie/dewey.html

Reynolds, M (1998) Reflection and Critical Reflection in Management Learning, Management Learning, Volume: 29 issue: 2, page(s): 183-200, https://doi.org/10.1177/1350507698292004, Accessed: 20/1/2018

Shermis, S. (1999) Reflective thought, critical thinking, Eric Digest, http://www.indiana.edu/~eric_rec/ieo/digests/d143.html Accessed: 10/1/2018

Schon, D. A. (1983). The reflective practitioner: How professionals think in action. New York: Basic Books.

Shorrab, A (2016) Reflection & Journey of Inspiration, Inspiration Forum, Bahrain.

Smyth, J (1989) Developing and Sustaining Critical Reflection in Teacher Education, Journal of Teacher Education, Volume: 40 issue: 2, page(s): 2-9, March 1. https://doi.org/10.1177/002248718904000202, Accessed: 10/1/2018

Turesky, Elizabeth Fisher; Gallagher, Dennis (June 2011). "Know thyself: coaching for leadership using Kolb's experiential learning theory" (PDF). *The Coaching Psychologist* 7: 5–14.

Teekman, B and Rgon, M (2000) Exploring reflective thinking in nursing practice. Vol 31, Issue 5, May, pp.1125–1135.

CHAPTER 7

Understanding Mechanisms of Resilience Economy- Live Application on a Complex Business Model[7]

Introduction

The concept of 'resilience' was first adopted within systems ecology in the 1970s, where it ignited the research of the cybernetics along with the complex systems theory. Resilience today became an operational strategy and part of many risk and development management programs.

Resilience Economy (RE) is a new concept and field that is still in its early exploration, and itsfocuses on balancing the welfare impact whether in time of peace and disaster. Therefore, RE does not only depend on the physical characteristics of the event or its direct impacts in terms of lost lives and assets. (Duval and Vogel, 2008; Rose, 2004).

---

[7] Buheji, M. (2017) Understanding Mechanisms of Resilience Economy- Live Application on a Complex Business Model. Advances, **Social Sciences Research Journal**, 4(14), pp. 52-64.

RE mechanisms targets to establish welfare impacts in the business model which depend on the ability of the economy to cope, recover, and reconstruct and therefore to minimise consumption losses. This ability that RE builds in the business models can be referred to as the microeconomic resilience. (Duval and Vogel, 2008).

This study would try to understand from the literature review the influence that the mechanisms of RE can bring in the different business models and especially in complex one and then explore how this has been used during inspiration labs that brought a major improvement to the reservation and conservation of a country essential natural resources, that water. (Fernandez, 2006).

The chapter discusses the economic resilience from different relevant points as culture and environment and what learnings can be taken relevant to 'stability'. Particular resilience practices are focused on as resilience in decision making, material diversity, investigations resilience, social integration and resilience towards sustainability in natural resources which is the focus of the context of the study.

Literature Review

Definition of Resilience

"Resilience" is about the ability to absorb shocks while continuing to function. It's a word that has gained a lot of currency in recent years as more and more people realize that they have some big shocks headed their way: financial shocks, energy shocks, environmental shocks, as social unrest and international conflict Rose (2004).

So resilience focus on the mental and then the physical ability to recover quickly from depression, illness or misfortune. The physical property of a material that can resume its shape after being stretched or deformed; elasticity. The positive ability of a system or company to adapt itself to the consequences of a catastrophic failure caused by a power outage, a fire, a bomb or similar (particularly IT systems, archives). While the word resilient means are able to endure, be bendable, be flexible, be strong without cracking, or with high ability to manage the impact of tribulation.

Resilience means human would be more ready to act as humans where mistakes are prone; however, management of mistakes is what they should be ready for.

Resilience and Persistence

Resilience needs persistence, which is a continuance course of action despite difficulty or opposition. Persistence builds the ability to recover from misfortune or change. Perrings, C. (1998) Collaborative work between ecologists and economists has used the ecological concept of resilience to explore the relative persistence of different states of nature. The concept of resilience has two main variants. One is concerned with the time taken for a disturbed system to return to some initial state and is due to Pimm (1984). A second is concerned with the magnitude of disturbance that can be absorbed before a system flips from one state to another and is due to Holling (1986).

Understanding Resilience from Nature

The ecological concept of resilience focus on change in economy-environment systems. The linkages between resilience and the stability of dynamical systems as biodiversity and the sustainability of alternative states. Walker and Cooper (2011).

Recent developments in modelling the resilience of joint economy-environment systems suggest the advantages of analysing the change in the system as a Markov process, the transition probabilities between states offering a natural measure of the resilience of the system in such states. It is argued that this 'emergent property' of the collaboration between ecology and economics has far-reaching implications for the way individuals think about, model and manage the environmental sustainability of economic development (Duval and Vogel, 2008).

Resilience and Adaptation

Resilience reflects a consensus about the necessity of adaptation through an endogenous crisis (Wong-Parodi et al., 2015). The generalisation of complex systems theory as a methodology of power has ambivalent sources. While the redefinition of the concept can be directly traced to the work of the ecologist Crawford S. Holling (1986), the deployment of complex systems theory is perfectly in accord with the later philosophy of the Austrian neoliberal Friedrich Hayek.

Since resilience deals with aspects of stability and adaptation, it offers then system equilibria, thus offering alternative measures in relevance to enhancing the capacity of a system to retain productivity following disturbance. This support the IE main requirement, i.e. the ability to shift towards capacity vs demand. Levin et al. (1998). Therefore, resilience became an enabler for managing the diversity in the Work Place and in managing the endogenous integration within the society.

Resilience in Business Models

Birchall (2009) focused on the importance of resilience designs in the business models to minimise economic crisis and improve the positive impact; using cooperative enterprises as a reference.

Birchall showed how the consumer, worker and financial cooperative models all remained financially sound; reporting an increased turnover and growth despite the high economic instability. (Nsouli, 1995).

Birchall showed how the cooperative model of enterprise not only survives the crisis, but also able to withstand crisis, maintaining the livelihoods of the communities in which they operate.

Therefore, establishing a resilience in business models can contribute to the organisations' inspiration and effectiveness since it raises its ability to undermined changes in the internal and external environment in a very efficient way as mentioned by Sosna et al. (2010).

Sosna and his team showed that resilience mechanisms built in business models of Spanish dietary products that were threatened by economic recession and heightened competition lead to help the business flourish and survive more and more. Resilience in the model of the dietary organisation made it outperform its competitors by a wide margin.

Resilience in the business model means that it builds a model that would meet high challenges and different life problems. It is a model that needs positive behaviour in meeting challenges which leads to increasing the capacity to demands. The role of the model is also a source of inspiration and directly or indirectly improve the overall socio-economic development. The model should help to ignite sustained feeling inspiration where it can be a point of reference for RE, as shown in Figure (1).

Figure (1) Components of a Resilience
Economy Business Model

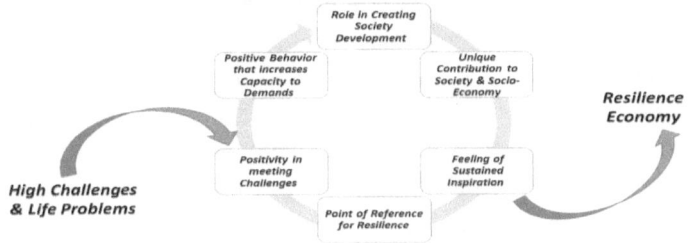

Demand for Resilience Mechanisms in Our Societies

Resilience mechanisms are rarely discussed in the literature, even though it is highly demanded all types of sectors and business in our societies and communities. Whatever the social status, the level of civilisation and type of social fabric, resilience mechanisms can play a significant role in creating a better outcome with minimal resources. Resilience in the designs of business models is highly needed today for the mindset of the middle class and decision makers in our societies, or those individuals responsible for the community services and development.

There many factors that influence the identification of the type of resilience needed in the business model, one of this factor is the problem that trigger the need for establishing a resilient mechanism. Therefore, there is a need to determine the particular behaviour of resilience that can be used to deal with the social problem.

Introduction Resilience Economy

RE is spreading more and more in different disciplines research such as in politics, economics, technology, finance, urban and environmental issues, security, social problems, psychology, problem-solving, legal issues and policy management (Kumpfer, 1999). RE requires identifying the scope of the business model in relevance to its socio-economic role, through recognising or analysing the model problem or challenges.

RE is much related to IE as mentioned in the work of Buheji (2016). RE requires restoration and adaptation while IE focuses on adoption and innovative development with minimal resource. Please refer to Figure (2)

Figure (2) Relation of Resilience Economy
and Inspiration Economy

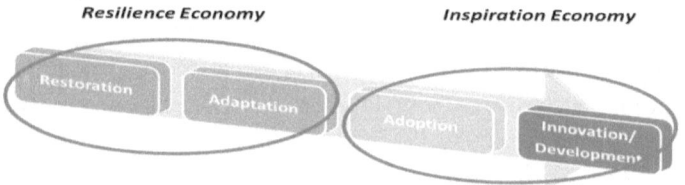

RE focus on managing the deviations in the socio-economic mechanisms. Non-Resilience is considered a weakness is the business model and it is an abnormal state because it does not reflect the social aspect of humanity.

RE focus on studying the business model that lead to the current living conditions of poor immigrants. For example, there is a need for more resilience practices from Europeans, who accepting African and Asian migrants every day in their countries and where those migrant are settling in urban cities that are known for their social mobility. There is a need for resilience practices in dealing with people from the underdeveloped areas of the Slums, where deep poverty, crime, delinquency, rift families and ethnic strife are preventing youth from seeing their dreams possible or achievable.

Same applies in the issue of dealing with the business model that guarantees the sustainability of essential water and energy supply. The business model needs to be resilient enough to minimise energy or water loss, while maintaining continuity of services. R, therefore, aims to study the deviant behaviour and identify the social problem and then find means to solutions that would help develop the socio-economic status.

Business Model Resilience and Deviant Behaviour

When individuals realise the existence of a business model problem they are working on, they take different and varied positions towards this. The positions of each differ according to the degree of proximity or distance from the problem. Their ability shift to focus on distancing themselves from the problem; instead of deeply understanding the opportunities of resilience in the model itself. (World Bank, 2013).

Since resilience is about mitigation and management of feelings or practices that lead to the indifference, people need to control their attitudes and practices in a way that would enhance the business model resilience.

In almost every type of speciality when the industrialisation and urbanisation increase the socio-economic problems increases in a very disorganised and deviant way that affects human behaviour and the way, the business model is delivered. This applies even to water utility services which are the context of this chapter.

The resilience mechanism helps to build socio-economic disintegration in the business model between the concerned parties, thus establishing Total People Involvement that would undergo with the value system in the community targeted.

Resilience is considered a compact against any socio-economic disintegration that leads to more dependence on specific resources in the business model. Resilient models do not mean conforming to the standards and values of the community, but it is about the ability to adapt. For example, building RE model in order to manage the issue of migration from south to north would need more resilience in the education of immigrants to solve their problems by creating for them mindsets that would build self-fulfilment supported by mentorship and educational programs.

The concept of perverse behaviour refers to a deviation from causes of consistent behaviour. The behaviour of an incompatible business model usually creates a challenge to the legitimacy of social norms. Resilience can overcome the uncoordinated business processes efforts which lead to behaviourally deviant practices.

Resilient models prevent the interference between socio-economic problems, deviation and disintegration. With resilient models, all sources of frustrations would be dealt with as early as possible to avoid reaching disintegration breaks out.

From Unstable Socio-Economy Practices to Resilience Economy Mechanisms

Today more than ever before there is a need for resilience mechanism to make our communities readier to be challenged as opposed to what might be learned from interaction and from challenging the current state of our lives. RE mechanisms focus on the classification of the business model problems that an organisation or a community faces towards a pattern of stability adaptation.

In order to shift from unstable socio-economy to a resilient economy, there is a need first to deal with the set of recurrent problems resulting from adapting to the external environment. To direct the outcome of the set of problems to satisfy the different business model component needs.

In order also to shift from unstable socio-economy there is a need to build mechanisms that turn the negative effect of the problems to a positive one. This would eliminate gradually the negative behaviour that demands confrontation and increases the probabilities for achieving the model stability, as illustrated in Figure (3).

Figure (3) Shifting from Unstable to Resilience Economy

In order to build resilience in the business model people need to be more aware of the problem, the clearer the problem becomes the more it can create a transformation from unstable socio-economy to a RE. The resilience mechanisms should help overcome problems and overcome the possibility of any mental rejection.

Therefore business models problems can be classified into fundamental business model problems linked to the lack of basic failure to deliver services or products relevant to the core of the business model, or non-satisfactory business model problems, or synergetic business model problem that is linked to the bad relations between different stakeholders of business model or the problem.

Mohamed Buheji & Dunya Ahmed

Role of Resilience Economy in Managing Complex Models

The resilience practices help to mitigate the level of problems in the business model. Resilience mechanisms can mitigate the strong impact of problems on the surrounding socio-economic conditions, or minimise the adverse conditions and results that are mainly caused by socio-economic problem affects, or reduce the harmful conditions which are directly or indirectly the product of the socio-economic problems on the business model.

RE mechanisms help to manage the challenges caused by the vulnerability of problem failures and raise the targeted business model adaptive capacity, as Figure (4) shows. The larger the population density that the business model applies for, the more complex the problem becomes and the more diverse its causes and sources, and the more its forms and types Röhnet al. (2015).

Figure (4) Role of Resilience in Managing Challenges

With the spirit persistence and the mechanisms of resilience, the creation of successful business models even in complex environment is highly possible as this leads to the greater insight that, in turn, leads to new waves of seeing hidden opportunities (Buheji, 2016). Once this resilience is established in the targeted culture, the inspiration starts to enhance our abilities to see solutions inside each difficulty, thus helping us to focus on sustained resilient models outcomes.

Creating inspired RE business models need to maintain the diversity of solutions with high levels of communication. This establishes resilient business models that can apply a formula for the sustenance of change. Complex business model, need to go through four stages, as shown in Figure (5). The first stage concerns going through a shift in cultural focus from 'what is wrong' to 'what works' in the business model. This means the need to be more resilient in terms of observing and discovering. Once it can absorb, opportunities of resilience better outcomes can be generated.

Figure (5) Journey of Resilience in the Inspiration Labs

Resilient in Observing & Discovering   *Resilient in Absorbing through Team*   *Resilient in Development*   *Resilient in Sustaining & Generalising Outcome*

- Capturing Opportunities
- Understanding Challenges
- Working on developing the Model
- Reflect & Celebrate Inspiration of Youth Economy

Development of Resilience Economy Mindset through Inspiration Engineering

Studies show that the business model is healthy (with high communication) and is profitable (with high value added) practices. The healthier and profitable the business model is the more its mechanisms would be resilient. Stability that will lead to acceptance; this establishes the first cycle in learning resilience. Moving towards greater sustainability, will feel the importance of abundance thinking.

Resilient mindsets will develop individuals and communities that are cooperative and self-sufficient, self-initiated and proactive (Birchall, 2009). Moreover, resilient mindsets lead to more positive thinking, making it more likely to be risk takers with a high ability to manage uncertainties. This is shown in Figure (6).

Figure (6) Characteristics of a Resilient Mindset

Therefore, it could be said that resilience mechanism creates an inspirational edge in the business model. Once the resilience of the model is started change agents are needed. The spirit of resilience can establish research and development clusters within the organisation. It can deliver more focused goodwill working practices that are reflected in the socio-economic business model outcome.

At the start of the process of observations and exploring opportunities in the business model, the capacity for resilience automatically raised. Ability to absorb what is learned during the exploration stages will increase our ability to find more opportunities thus enhancing our knowledge and inspiration sources. (Buheji, 2006).

Synthesise and absorb the results of observation, will let it start to shift towards a new realisation of 'what can be done' to change and develop our mindsets about the business model, as illustrated in Figure (7).

Figure (7) Capacity for Business Model Resilience during after the Inspiration Lab and its Role in Changing Mind-sets

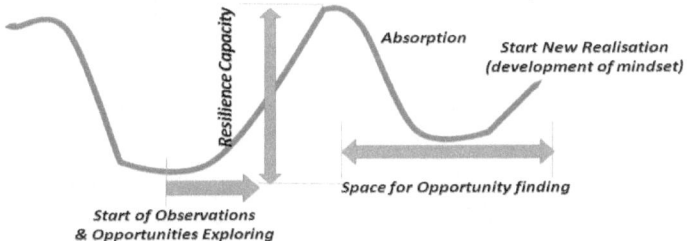

Reivich and Shatte (2003), authors of 'Resilience Factor', found that overcoming life's hurdles requires us to break down a problem into parts and determine which one can be solved first; then fix what can be fixed and then let the rest go. Resilience in Inspiration Labs is developed gradually based on this practice. Through practising more and more, the capturing of opportunities, understanding the challenges, and working on the development of a model, can reflect and learn from the inspiration journey.

With the presence of resilience absorption techniques, the amplification of the problem is in control, thus to avoid reaching a situation where the general public works on their discontent and discomfort. RE can mitigate the possibility of amplification of the problem and minimise its size and effects in a way that the reformers can easily handle it.

Mohamed Buheji & Dunya Ahmed

Methodology

The research methodology employed in this chapter is a qualitative case study. The case study was chosen as a method because it is suitable for situations that include complex and multiple variables and processes (Yin, 2003). A longitudinal case study that was carried over a period of 6 months examined the complex business model of water production management in the kingdom of Bahrain. With this kind of qualitative method, it was essential to capture the resilience mechanisms used during the inspiration lab that lead to creating a RE compliant business model is relevant to water production with minimal water loss.

The case study enabled an investigation into real-life events about specific evidence of resilience practices that started with interviews and observations. The chapter attempts to address the research question: "How can RE Mechanisms work to inspire complex Business Models?', i.e. ensuring the transformation of the model to be more robust and agile.

As is typical in case studies (Meredith, 1998), the case data were collected from multiple sources: thematic discussions, workshops and interviews with water authority representatives, besides concerned stakeholders. Following the principles of action research, the researcher and the actors in the case wanted to solve the urgent, immediate problem of the business model, and this reflected on the development of the process of problem-solving and great experiential learning teamwork.

The interviews and trial and error field testing under what is called inspiration labs helped to get the water authority decision makers and key stakeholders more attached to the development of a better business model that handles water loss in a country that is surrounded by sea and with no sweat water except the little remaining wells.

The business model of water production and supply directorate was based on the supply of pure water from main stations to every consumer in the most efficient way, i.e. with minimal loss. Through Inspiration Engineering and Labs and unique approaches in problem-solving resilient business model was pushed with the purpose to minimise the water loss even with the fast expansion of the water network system, due to boom in population.

In this case, the socio-economic issue was minimising loss of the 40% leakage in the utility water supply network by inspiring the water authority as an organisation and enhancing its teams' ability to discover early underground leakages and losses through observation and forecasting, and then by applying a level of intelligent decision making. The techniques went through the following main steps in order to gradually enhance the mechanisms of economic resilience in the water authority business model:

Step (1) Understanding the Problem to be Solved

Starting any problem solving cannot be without understanding what is the essence of the problem, i.e. realising the amount of water loss in the country because of system leakage between the source (the main water desalination stations) and delivery points (customers' water input points); despite the increase in the maintenance budget for water pipes and the overall water network.

Step (2): Realising the impact of the problem on natural resources in the future.

Start by understanding the taxonomy of 'water loss' and its differentiation from 'water leakage', then applying this differentiation to check the difference.

Step (3): Outline the Scientific Method for Problem Solving

In order to outline the problem, there is a need to start setting proper resilience analysis of the business model and how the water

authority handles the water leakage incidents and accidents by asking the participating teams to:
a) Codify the type of water loss and leakage.
b) Classify the categories of water loss and leakage in terms of place, time, type of area, pipe designs and detection equipment.
c) Specifying the relation and the correlation between seen (visible) and hidden (invisible) water loss (both from an analysis of previous history and field observations).

Step (4): Studying Attitudes in terms of Inspiration Economy Requirements

Without understanding the attitudes towards the business model problem cannot be solved; thus in this stage, there is a need to start:
- Identify the types of emergency readiness relevant to stopping water loss (both the seen and the hidden).
- Identify the average length of time taken to rectify a loss of water by type and area, besides the type of field response team needed.
- Understand all the challenges in compacting water loss and leakage as regards the type and amount of consumer areas, the age of the water network, the level of consumption, the type of real estate (i.e. normal domestic consumer, public consumer or a private company, etc.).

Step (5): Start Reasoning about the Problem to ease the Complexity of the Water Supply Business Model (by Applying Suitable Convergent and Divergent Thinking Approaches).

Using both convergent and divergent thinking is very important for creating an opportunity from a challenge or a problem. In order to achieve this, there is a need to:
- Start reasoning the type and amount of water leakage by the level of building heights and the size of the population.

- Use reasoning to re-engineer the process of water loss and water leakage, and the way this impact the response team readiness. This should help to identify and then remove the non-value-added steps.
- Train, drill and deploy teams to effectively isolate the area network from the main water supply network.
- Enhance water loss detection equipment in areas that are prone to experience hidden water loss due to their history, type of design, and forecast data.
- Start piloting projects in three main areas/types of water consumer: old areas, new areas, large consumers.

Step (6): Start Re-phrasing the Problem

In order to solve a complex problem, there is a need to re-phrase it, by:
- Categorise the type of challenges in each area and segregate the issues of illegal connections that count for part of the water loss problem.
- Design specific water pipes for tight areas which would be unique in size and thickness; these include characteristics to make them flexible yet robust.

Step (7): Reducing the Problem's Complexity

Both the business model and the problem complexity were reduced throughout the inspiration lab journey in order to create a more resilient economy model through:
- Understanding the types of defect in water meters that lead to slow detection and hence slow response of the emergency team.
- Understanding the places where leakage occurs inside houses and study trends or repetitions in terms of the types of connection.

- Building a 'Water Loss Intelligence Programme' that will enhance (i.e. inspire) the Water Authority to respond proactively to potential water loss on time and with high availability, better efficiency, and more effectively.
- Applying a 'Mitigation of Risks Programme' to support the 'Water Loss Intelligence Programme'.

This project helped to reduce the business model complexity and make it more resilient and also reduced the country water loss by 30%. The details of the numbers of all the above were removed to maintain confidentiality.

Discussion and Conclusion

Working on applying RE mechanisms on critical national issues as significant water loss could be a very strong technique to handle complex business models of different nature. With resilience mechanisms focused on business models development and problem-solving can improve the welfare impacts on many types of socio-economic issues. Micro-economic resilience, can manage the distribution of losses or mitigate causes of vulnerability. When systems are economically resilient, it would be more ready to mitigate risks and absorb shocks.

In a resilient economy improved business models can influence positively more the socio-economy and enhance the learning outcome. The learnings from the water authority loss and leakage case study are that business models can be far more resilient if it focuses on its socio-economic system and works on to compensate its immediate losses, however complex it is. Therefore, it is advised that more research work is done to freely generalise the importance of resilient economy mechanisms and its ability to minimise welfare losses for any business model regardless of its given magnitude.

Reference

Birchall, J (2009) Resilience of the Cooperative Business Model in Times of Crisis, International Labour Organisation http://www.ilo.org/empent/Publications/WCMS_108416/lang--en/index.htm

Buheji, M (2016) Handbook of Inspiration Economy. Bookboon. ISBN: 978-87-403-1318-5. http://bookboon.com/en/handbook-of-inspiration-economy-ebook

Duval, R. and L. Vogel, (2008) Economic resilience to shocks. The role of structural policies, OECD

Fernandez, R (2016) 5 Ways to Boost Your Resilience at Work, Harvard Business Review, June.

Hill, E; Wial, H and Wolman, H (2008) Exploring Regional Economic Resilience, Working Paper, Institute of Urban and Regional Development. https://www.econstor.eu/handle/10419/59420

Holling CS (1986) Resilience and stability of ecological systems. Annual Review of Ecology and Systematics 4: 1–23.

Holling CS (1986) Resilience of ecosystems: Local surprise and global change. In: Clark WC, Munn RE (eds) Sustainable Development of the Biosphere: Cambridge: Cambridge University Press, 292–317.

Hurdles, Harmony; Reprint edition (October 14, 2003) Keys to Finding Your Inner Strength and Overcoming Life's

Kumpfer, K (1999) The Resilience Framework, Factors and Processes Contributing to Resilience, Resilience and Development. Part of the series Longitudinal Research in the Social and Behavioral Sciences: An Interdisciplinary Series, pp 179-224.

Lange O (1949) The practice of economic planning and the optimum allocation of resources. Econometrica 17: 166–171.

Nsouli SM, (eds) (1995) Resilience and growth through sustained adjustment: The Moroccan experience. International

Monetary Fund Occasional Paper No. 117. Washington, DC: International Monetary Fund.

Perrings, C. (1998) Resilience in the Dynamics of Economy-Environment Systems, Environmental Resource Economical, Vol. 11 (3-4): pp. 503-520.

Reivich, K and Shattle, A (2003) The Resilience Factor: 7

Röhn, O., A. Caldera Sánchez, M. Hermansen and M. Rasmussen, (2015) Economic resilience: A new set of vulnerability indicators for OECD countries, OECD Economics Department Working Papers, No. 1249, OECD Publishing, Paris.

Rose, A (2004) Defining and measuring economic resilience to disasters, Disaster Prevention and Management: An International Journal, Vol. 13 Issue: 4, pp.307-314, https://doi.org/10.1108/09653560410556528

Sondermann, D (2016) Towards more resilient economies:

Sosna, M; Nelly, R; Rodriguez, T; Velamuri, S (2010) Business Model Innovation through Trial-and-Error Learning: The Naturhouse Case, Long Range Planning, Volume 43, Issues 2–3, April–June 2010, Pages 383-407

The role of well-functioning economic structures, Reports No. 1984 November, European Central Bank, Working Paper.

Walker, J and Cooper, M (2011) Genealogies of Resilience,

Washington, DC: World Bank.

Wong-Parodi, G; Fischhoff, B; Strauss, B (2015) Resilience vs. Adaptation: Framing and action, Climate Risk Management 10: 1–7.

World Bank (2013) World Development Report 2014: Risk and Opportunity—Managing Risk for Development,

Yin, R. (2003) Case Study Research, Third Edition Sage

CHAPTER 8

Youth Unemployment Mitigation Labs "An Empathetic Approach for Complex Socio-Economic Problem"[8]

Introduction

Youth unemployment would continue to be a complicated problem as the world is continuing its demographic shifts in developing countries. The problem of youth unemployment will continue to carry numerous domestic and global risks, including social exclusion, mass migration and generational gaps. Buheji (2018d). At a time when young people in certain societies are being prepared as the engine of society and its sustainable resource.

Youth unemployment needs an economic, social and psychological approach more than a political approach. It is a security problem that carries with deep consequences towards poverty, deprivation and frustrations which have profound effects on the level of quality of life of the community.

---

[8] Buheji, M. (2019) Youth Unemployment Mitigation Labs "An Empathetic Approach for Complex Socio-Economic Problem" American Journal of Economics,9(3) 93-105.

Unemployment effects both the psychological and the physical status of youth more than ever today. Studies show that the effects of unemployment stem from a sense of failure and loss of self-esteem, which raises the rate of silence that may lead some to commit a crime, drug abuse and even suicide.

In this chapter, we shall explore the meaning of unemployment for youth specifically, besides modern unemployment statistics. Youth unemployment as a problem to be solved is discussed from different perspectives such as the current and required such as education and recreation activities. Economic Discussion (2019).

Policies to reduce youth unemployment and the required policy reforms. Then a review for those youth not in education, not in employment and not in training, called for short (NEET). Then a review about the role of knowledge-based economy on the issue of youth unemployment is followed. Examples of youth unemployment challenges and the probability of youth staying unemployed shed light on the depth and the complexity of the problem. Buheji (2018e).

Then a case study of the way inspiration labs is tackling the youth unemployment a socio-economic problem and from different perspectives is explored. A comparative discussion on the contemporary efforts in tackling the youth unemployment issue in relevance to inspiration is evaluated and discussed, then recommendations for the way forward to close this major UN-SDG gap are suggested in conclusion. Amadeo (2018).

Literature Review

What is Youth Unemployment?

Unemployment can be defined as when an individual is hunting for employment and does not find a job or alternatives to a job, i.e. being self-employed. Unemployment is one of the major crisis that happens around the world every era. Therefore, it is an issue that reflects the national or international economic status and the healthiness of investment potentials. Johansson and Handelshögskolan (2015).

The unemployment rate is measured by calculating the total unemployed individuals divided by the total number of the labour force in the country. As per the International Labour Organization (ILO,2012), there are more than 200 million globally or about 6% of the complete world workforce is unemployed. For youth, their unemployment differs even more if their NEET is high. I.e. When youth are not in education and not work means we have a society a major wastage of both youth energy and spirit, Buheji (2018d).

Youth Unemployment Statistics

Statistics of Youth Unemployment in Modern History

The global unemployment rate reached a post during World War II to a high of 9.7% in 1982. With the economic recession, the unemployment rate reached 9.6% in the year 1983. It was in 1989 that the unemployment rate dropped to 5% but started enhancing again. This led to 6.8% in 1991 and 7.5% in 1992. Later and with the economic development, the unemployment rate fell to 6.9% in 1993, 4.5% in 1998 and to 4% in 2000; consequently. It was considered to be the lowest in the last three decades.

Since youth are essential to any economic development and growth, the drop down in the overall global unemployment rate gave great hope for the ease of young people entry to the labour market, especially in emerging and developing market economies. This is especially true as the world reach approximately one-third of its working-age being youth. Buheji (2018d), Lagard and Bludorn (2019).

However, the reality today is the opposite. Still today youth, all over the world, face tough labour markets and job shortages. Approximately, 20% of 15- to 24-year-olds in the average emerging market and the developing economy are neither in work, nor in school (i.e. NEET); in comparison to 10% in advanced economies. Table (1) illustrates the percentage of youth unemployment selected developed and emerging economy countries, as per ILO (2015) statistics.

Table (1) Shows Youth Unemployment by Country

Country	% Youth Unemployment
Australia	13.2
Greece	50.6
France	25.4
India	18.1
Italy	43.9
Japan	7.2
Poland	23.2
South Korea	8.7
Spain	53.5
Turkey	19.5
United Kingdom	16.3
United States	12.4

Source: ILO 2015

The International Monetary Fund (IMF) published a report in (2019) that show that the share of youth, i.e. ages of 15-24 years, NEET in the past 13 years (from 2003 till 2016) stayed within 25-20% in emerging markets and developing countries, while in developed countries it stayed within 10%. Ahn et al. (2019) and Lagard and Bludorn (2019).

In Africa, youth unemployment is one of the growing problems in the continent and the world. It is of high importance, even more, today due to the migration crisis. According to the International Labour Organization (ILO), the unemployment rate among youth in Northern Africa was at 29.3% in 2016. (ILO, 2016). The situation in sub-Saharan Africa, specifically, is only slightly better where the youth unemployment rate was at 10.8% last year. In South Africa, more than half of all active youth were unemployed in 2016, representing the highest youth unemployment rate in the region. Buheji (2017b).

In Europe, the numbers are even worse. In general youth unemployment rates have reached in certain countries about 50% on average. For example, in Spain youth unemployment rates reached (53.7%) and in Greece (50.7%), in Italy (42.9%), in Croatia (41.8%), in Portugal (35.5%), in Cyprus (34.9%) and Slovakia (28.5%). The lowest shown youth unemployment rate is in France (24.4%), then in Ireland (23.8%) and the same in Belgium.

World Economic Forum (WEF) (2018) report warned that such sustained global financial crisis would create a "lost generation" and would hinder youth integration into traditional patterns of economic life. Among the specific issues raised by WEF report were the long-term youth unemployment; low-quality, part-time and temporary employment jobs. The WEF also pointed out the risk of weak links between education and worked; the impact of demographic change and migration; and the increasing pressures in relevance to social protection (WEF, 2019).

WEF (2018) shows that youth unemployment has been broadly static since the publication of the WEF 2014 report, i.e. before the global financial crisis. Even where jobs creation has picked up since the crisis, concerns are rising about the growing prevalence of low-quality employment and the rise of the "gig economy".

In 2016, the UN launched the 'global initiative for decent jobs for youth' to coordinate policies on youth employment and young people's labour rights. The EU released €6 billion, as a youth jobs guarantee program, targeting to ensure that within four months of becoming unemployed young people are offered new employment, education, or a workplace apprenticeship.

Future Foresight of Youth Unemployment

Predictions say that youth unemployment will continue to rise in the following years. High unemployment has negative consequences on the economy of the country and population. More young people are expected to leave their countries of birth to find employment abroad.

The new IMF staff study shows that, if youth underemployment in the typical emerging market and developing economy were brought in line with the average advanced economy, the working-age employment rate would rise by three percentage points and economic output would get a 5% boost. IMF (2019) and Lagard and Bludorn (2019).

Youth Unemployment - Problems Solving

Youth Unemployment as a Problem

Unemployment as a problem can be solved in many ways and alternatives. Solving youth unemployment as a socio-economic problem can help to reduce the current total approaches of youth empowerment, Amadeo (2018). Most current approaches work to solve long-term youth unemployment is through ensuring better educational standards, launching of new empowerment programs, encouraging self-employment, entrepreneurship, ensuring access to basic education and reduction of the age of retirement. Buheji (2018a, 2018e).

Recently, most of the scientists see unemployment as an issue that could be solved when youth become creative, positive and competitive. This led to many initiatives that target to avoiding investing in unsuitable programs. Buheji (2018d). Youth unemployment is another issue which is still happening in developed, underdeveloped and developing countries. There is significant evidence that even the developed countries are battling with youth unemployment issues. The international labour organisation has mentioned the statistics of both employed and unemployed in 2012 which states that is about 6% of the world population are unemployed and youths are the ones who are unemployed, i.e. youth unemployment (ILO, 2012).

Many studies now show clear evidence that the delay in youth unemployment increases their likelihood of being unemployed in their later adult life (Gregg, 2001; Bell and Blanchflower, 2009). As a result, youth unemployment will also have a sustained impact on the level of wealth and growth in future periods.

Now officially EU sees youth unemployment to be a serious problem even in Europe where the Eurostat (2015) shows the unemployed youth to be 22.1%, compared to 8.9% for the adult population. This figure shows the considerable difficulties that young people are facing when trying to access the labour market for the first time.

Education and Unemployment Problem

Education creates opportunities for young people that contribute to the fulfilment of their desires and the building of their personalities and the establishment of a secure and stable life. Education supposed to facilitate a better search for suitable jobs and opens the youth mindset to see opportunities in different ways. Therefore, many believe with their education certificates they would get open doors of opportunities. Buheji, (2017c), WEF (2019).

The government should change the policies of requiring an expensive bachelor's degree, that take four to five years of one's life without real guaranteed employment outcome. Students should have more options to go to vocational school, or get a combination of liberal arts and then on-the-job training. Hence, it would be great to see companies start adopting apprenticeship programs, teaching young professionals what they need to know on the job. Ahn et al. (2019), Buheji (2018b), Buheji (2017a).

Boosting on human capital education and training are no longer an effective strategy to create employable youth, or labour productivity, nor does keeping high demand for the creation of new jobs. Reddy (2017). Part of the EU recent initiatives also is to improve educational attainment so that people can work in jobs requiring higher-level knowledge and skills. EU and national policies aimed at reducing school drop-out rates. WEF (2019).

The Active Labour Market Policy (ALMP) target to support youth employment and 'youth guarantee' schemes to ensure young people receive a job offer or continued education within a fixed period after leaving education, or becoming unemployed (European Commission 2014). This is supported with extended guidance to employment services created specifically to youth. This is also linked now to employers' social contributions (O'Higgins, 2010; Eurofound, 2011).

Now many students graduate with education fees debts on their shoulder. Lack of diversified educational models that address the different youth vs market demands needs to lead to staying in confusion in the search for work and waiting for more than ten years without suitable or permanent work. The constraints for specialisation increases the complexity of the problem of unemployment.

Despite their differentiated access to education, studies show that youth still suffer from inequality for jobs related to their welfare. Total unemployment could be valued at market prices, for example using young people's wage levels and average working hours, to provide a measure of wealth lost to the EU economy, because of youth underemployment in the same present period. For example, a recent Eurofound study has shown the estimated cost of young people who are NEETs in 26 of EU member states to be about €156 billion (representing 1.51% of EU's GDP) (Eurofound, 2012).

To reducing youth occupational immobility, many countries started apprenticeship schemes that aim to provide the unemployed youth with the suitable skills they need to find suitable employment and to make them attractive for a suitable job. For example, in 2013, over 500,000 people started apprenticeships in the UK.

Consistent with the increase in education is the decrease in the share of 16-21 year-olds in fulltime work (Barham, et al., 2009). Further, the evidence-base on particular transitions examines the impact of the constant growth of young people in temporary employment across the EU. This increased to about 42% of young people across the EU in 2010, compared to about 11% of those aged 25–59 (Eurofound, 2014).

The recent (EU Commission, 2014) report shows the increased focus on improving the skills of young people to meet employers' demands better and to reduce the mismatch between available vacancies and job seekers by supporting vocational learning in apprenticeships, traineeships and placements and introducing quality standards for vocational education. Thus funding more apprenticeships and workplace learning are now a top priority for EU countries (EMCO, 2011; ILO, 2011; O'Higgins, 2010; European Employment Observatory, 2010).

Youth Sport and Unemployment Problem

Today youth-focused sports contribute to absorbing the burdens of disturbance resulting from unemployment disruption. By integrating youth into a social and cultural atmosphere, while contributing to the building of youth's personality and spirituality we can transform the energy into balanced and productive work, thus preventing deviation and mental illness.

Through Improving the situation of many millions of young Europeans failing to find gainful employment, and more generally suffering from deprivation and social exclusion, has to be a priority for policy-makers' initiatives.

Influence of Youth Unemployment Problem

The problem of youth unemployment can influence the stability of national insurance contributions to society. The level of financial support expenditure for apprenticeships and internships would be influenced too.

Employed youth can reduce occupational mobility and thus knowledge capital leakage. Also, a well-established employment program would help to improve geographical mobility and thus to cause improvement for the minimum wages. Once youth are employed the community would avoid the risk of the poverty trap.

In 2012, 42.1% of young people across the EU were on a temporary contract which was four times the rate for adult workers (Eurofound, 2013). This shows the gap that youth unemployment does. Now it is an accepted trend and fact that full-employment does not mean zero unemployment! There will always be some frictional youth unemployment which may be useful to have a small surplus pool of labour available. Most economists argue that there will always be some frictional unemployment of perhaps 2-3% of the labour force.

Amadeo (2015) seen that economic growth rate of 2-3 per cent can create only a maximum of 150,000 jobs which is not enough to prevent high youth unemployment, especially with the high influx of graduates. When unemployment creeps above 6-7 % and stays there, it means the economy cannot create enough new youth jobs also.

Policies to Reduce Youth Unemployment

General Policies to Reduce Youth Unemployment

Many policies are usually released to reduce youth unemployment. For example, the low interest rates and improving credit supply to businesses, besides depreciation in the exchange rate to help exporters is part of the story. Other indirect youth unemployment policies were the infrastructure investment projects, reductions in corporation tax (to increase investment), spending more incentives for research and innovation that would encourage new business start-ups.

Most countries in the world have moved their policy to rapidly support small and medium enterprises (SME's) because of their inability to create new jobs. New policies now focus on SMEs approaches that target to transform the educated youth to be a major source of innovation and economic empowerment. Other policies, as the productive families' empowerment policy, helped to create the right conditions for youth to start their jobs as part of the family. Such policies help youth to create the right source of income and training to enter the labour market through self-employment projects. Buheji (2018a)

Recent EU reform policies and programmes (Eurofound 2012, Berlingieri et al. 2014, O'Reilly et al. 2015) aim to review the employment protection legislation in relevance to minimum wages to encourage companies to take on more young people. (Eurofound, 2011; O'Higgins, 2010).

Policies that Encourage Self-employment

Johansson and Handelshögskolan (2015) studied why some youth become self-employed instead of wage or salary earners upon returning to employment, using Finnish microdata and a multinomial logit model. To close the unemployment gap, the

European Union established a SALTO-YOUTH program which is a network of six resource centres working on European priority areas within the youth field. Hence, self-employment policies have shifted the focus of the government towards subsidising the cost of the new start-ups. European Union (2019).

As the dependency ratio is increasing in almost all the developed countries and leading developing countries, government policies need to re-evaluate its expenditures on social security or social insurance program and focus on empowering or developing youth for creating more their markets or meeting the demands of the dynamics of the market. Young people are highly needed today to enter the labour market as self-employed, as early as possible, as they can help in managing to pay for the huge numbers of those retiring Buheji (2018a).

Evans and Leighton (1989) report that the salary youth that has entered self-employment on average have more experience than those not entering self-employment. Studies indicate that in the U.S. youth that suffers from longer duration of unemployment were more likely to enter self-employment.

The more we have concrete self-employed projects that would help to reduce youth unemployment this would influence the functioning of the labour market and would enhance the investment of youth in education and development (European Commission 2014a and 2014b) and Johansson and Handelshögskolan (2015).

Key barriers to Lowering Unemployment

There are many key barriers to lowering the unemployment issue. For example, high levels of long-term youth structural unemployment in the UK was found to be due to the complex welfare benefits, or low paid jobs that keep families in relative poverty (WEF, 2019).

Studies show that one of the barriers of unemployment is that they are being stuck on part-time jobs. Other barrier found to be due to the continuous gap and variations in education outcomes or having low levels of educational achievements Ahn et al. (2019).

Other barriers to reducing unemployment are the inequality for young women who usually influenced by negative economic conditions more than young men. Parental education was found to affect young people's employment transitions significantly.

Youth NEET as part of the Unemployment Problem

NEET is very important to measure the effectiveness of youth employment approaches in any country or community. Although they remain in a precarious labour market status and at risk of social exclusion during their participation in such programmes, they would not be classified as NEET. For example, youth unemployment rates, despite being available for all EU member states, or rates of young people NEET as a percentage of the total resident population of the age group, depend to a large extent on the characteristics of the education system (Eurofound, 2012).

A study was carried in the UK, by the National Statistics Office (2016), showed that NEET is an issue in 90% of the member states starting with countries as France, Greece, Spain and Italy where its proportion ranges between 25% and 30% of young people who an immigrant/minority background, or living in disadvantaged areas. Many of these youth NEETs vary considerably across the EU between 4.4% of all young people in the Netherlands to 21.8% in Bulgaria (Eurofound, 2012).

Studies show that to manage the challenge of NEET, the school-to-work transition, need to be redesigned including the transition from further education colleges to the labour market, Crawford et al. (2011). Crawford and his team carried a similar longitudinal study on the UK and found generally that the trend of youth continuation in education enrolment of ages 16- to 21. However, the average youth employment rate slightly declined, and the use of fixed-term contracts increased, while the share of 16-year-olds who were not participating in education fell.

To improve the inclusion in the labour market and human capital accumulation while reducing segmentation and transitions from school to NEET; The European Commission has released selected indicators to monitor the field of youth NEET policy. A 'Dashboard of 40 EU Youth Indicators' (European Commission, 2011) was produced in March 2011, listing: Education/Training; Employment and Entrepreneurship; Health and Well-Being; Social Inclusion; Culture and Creativity; Youth Participation; Volunteering; Youth and The World.

2.7 Youth Unemployment as a Global Issue in Knowledge Economy

The issue of unemployment is very silly in an age with knowledge supposed to be the currency and new trend. It requires the cooperation of regional and national institutions, an in-depth analysis of the problem and the active participation of everyone. Although EU development in the knowledge-based economy; Quintini and Martin (2006) found that between 1995 and 2006 on average youth unemployment fell across OECD countries, however, it improved in more than half of the countries but severely deteriorated in a few.

Living in a digital age where modern communication technology has shaped our world, and it has impacted our lives tremendously and is supposed to solve the world's biggest problems. For example, Singularity University in the US is teaching people how to leverage exponential technology to impact 1 billion people positively. This is a knowledge-based era where youth impact can be tremendous if they are well utilised and appreciated. Economic Discussion (2019).

Hence, the more youth are employed with the mindset of minimising material consumption and focus on production that integrates knowledge in the output the more possibilities they are expected to get. Due to this change, intellectual labour youth is needed more today in the labour market to re-evaluate the productive age and help towards effective transformation. It is a generation that could benefit more from good technology infrastructure and highly connected mobility business with low-cost internet connections, if employed and their productivity optimised at the right time Buheji (2018c).

With youth continuing not to be employed in the right time and place, we would still have youth not being connected to mobile devices which means a greater loss of potential opportunities. Despite this fact, there are more than half a billion people across Africa now subscribe to mobile services, despite it being the highest continent in poverty. Buheji (2017c).

With the rapid evolution of the technology and the demand for a digitally skilled workforce, we call for short today the App generations, governments and education authorities need to adapt to the fast change based on this technology in the education system. This adaptation capacity would reflect on the compatibility of youth to the fast-changing market demands. Eshelman (2015), Buheji (2018b).

Examples of Youth Unemployment Challenges

To shed an example of the type of youth unemployment challenges, a review of the published literature about east, west and middle of the world was explored. In the United Kingdom, for example, youth employment found to happen only when there is sustained economic growth. Reducing cyclical volatility in relevance to youth requires a UK balanced growth. This found to effect even the education investment. In the USA, youth unemployment is three times ahead of the elders. The youth unemployment rate is above 5.7%, and about 17% of the nation's youth are jobless. WEF (2019).

In Korea, the study of Kim (2019) mentioned about the most sought-after careers among teenagers and young adults in South Korea are becoming government jobs. This is due to the slowing down of the Korean economic growth in export-driven industries. Kim mentioned about 10 million of graduating youth in the next five years are considering risk-free government jobs.

Unemployment among those Koreans of ages 15 to 29 reached 11.6% last spring. It is a level where the Korean president called to be catastrophic, compared what used to be between 3% and 4% just a few years ago. Analysts say part of the problem for young job seekers in South Korea is the widening gap between the quality of jobs at family-owned conglomerates like Samsung and LG and the rest of the players, due to global economic slow.

In Algeria, Yahia (2018) carried a study about the evolution of the unemployment rate and growth rate in Algeria during the period 1970- 2015. The overall unemployment rate in Algeria has declined considerably over the last decade falling from 28.3% in 2000 to 9.4% in 2015.

The first analysis indicates that this Algerian unemployment decline was due in particular to the public investment programmes implemented in the period 2000-2015. This public employment programs created about 6.25 million jobs between 1999 and 2008. This economic growth has probably contributed to the fall in youth unemployment, real GDP growth increased from 3% in 2001 to 7.2% in 2003 and 5.9% in 2005, followed by a sharp slowdown in 2006 and 2007 to around 1.7% and 1.6% respectively, partly because the surge in international oil prices affected domestic demand. Howeverm Yahia (2018) reported that the unemployment rate in Algeria (9.4% in 2015) remains high compared to other the Middle East and North Africa (MENA) countries. For instance, in 2014, the unemployment in Iran is 10.6%, Morocco 10.2%, Turkey 9.2%, MENA countries 8.8%, Venezuela 7%, Indonesia 6.2%, Saudi Arabia 5.6%, Russia 5.1%, China 4.7%, Nigeria 4.8%. Yahia (2018).

Hadjivassiliou et al. (2015) examined labour market performance affecting young people in the light of recent policies in Europe, drawing on an analysis of EU Labour Force Survey data 2004-2012. Hadjivassiliou and his colleagues developed a single index measure of labour market performance combining nine variables of labour market inclusion, human capital formation, labour market segmentation and transitions out of education. The idea was that one index would show the performance in relevance to employment capacity and especially youth. No EU Member States achieved full 100 per cent performance on individual dimensions, for example avoiding entirely unsuccessful transitions out of school or achieving full employment of the 15-24-year-olds. The index can be interpreted as measuring the shortfall of achievement across the four key dimensions of inclusion, human capital formation, labour market segmentation and transitions out of the education. Hence institutional change is needed to create effective outcomes in factors associated with young people's labour market transitions.

Probability of Youth Staying Unemployed

When we compare unemployed youth probability of moving into a wage or salary work with the probability of moving to self-employment, we find that married youth individuals, individuals with longer unemployment spells, individuals with more self-employment experience, and individuals with more wealth are more likely to become self-employed instead of taking a wage or salary job upon becoming reemployed. Johansson and Handelshögskolan (2015).

To anticipate the results, we find that a long spell of unemployment increases the probability of entering self-employment from unemployment when compared to entering paid employment from unemployment. This also holds after controlling for previous self-employment experience.

In countries with large-scale apprenticeship systems, such as Germany and Austria, youth have less possibility of staying unemployed. Youth apprentices are included in the total labour force, because vocational education and training (VET) are delivered primarily by firms.

However, unemployment as a percentage of the total labour force in countries with college-based VET is likely to be upward-biased because of the understated denominator (total labour force). In apprenticeship countries, youth unemployment probability risks are understated because the total labour force includes all people in VET.

Many youths have the right skills to find fresh work, but factors such as high house prices and housing rents, family and social ties and regional differences in the cost of living make it difficult and sometimes impossible to change the location to get a new job. Many economists point to a persistently low level of new house-building as a major factor impeding labour mobility and the chances of finding new work.

In order to reduce the possibility of youth staying unemployed for long times, many governments subsidies for businesses that take on the long-term unemployed – for example, as part of the UK youth contract, payments of up to £2,275 are available to employers who take on young people (aged 18-24) who have been claiming JSA for more than six months. The same thing in Bahrain was employed in specific industries would get more than half of the national youth salary for the first two years. In certain countries in Europe, there is a scheme that would help to lower the tax on businesses that employ more youth or support the employer national insurance contributions.

In the last one decade, many developing countries have started to follow the EU programs which encourage entrepreneurship and innovation as a way of creating new products and market demand which could generate new employment opportunities?

Methodology

Youth unemployment is a tragedy that is no one's fault in particular. It is a political problem. It is an economic problem. Moreover, it is a societal problem. Here are three solutions that try to tackle youth unemployment from a few different angles.

The current approaches for youth unemployment are synthesised to be either proactive or reactive approaches. Then these current approaches are compared to the published approaches of Inspiration Labs and how it addresses youth unemployment as a socio-economic problem. A holistic, practical solution is extracted from both the synthesis of the current literature and latest labs regarding mitigation of youth unemployment as a proactive way to avoid a foresighted crisis.

Case Study

The international inspiration economy project which started in September 2015 focused on different socio-economic problems, like poverty, women advancement, youth migration and quality of life. One of the repeated problems solved, through models only is the mitigation of youth unemployment, which is called 'Youth Unemployment Mitigation Labs'. The idea of these labs was to reduce youth unemployment or its negative influence through proactive models that could help to solve the complexity of this mega socio-economic problem. Buheji (2018e).

The following list of Table (2) shows the different socio-economic problems or challenges solved in relevance to youth unemployment and the mitigation approaches followed in the different communities, countries visited and in different situations.

Most of these socio-economic solutions have detailed stories behind them, as what is the causes of the youth unemployment and why and how it is created or influence; which is beyond the purpose of this chapter. Many of these projects were carried out in Bahrain, Bosnia & Herzegovina, Slovenia, Morocco, Mauritania and most recently in India. Hence, it cannot be compared to the many and long efforts of many countries in relevance to impact, however, it can be matched for the effectiveness of the approaches taken it is being new possibilities for closing the youth unemployment gap effectively and efficiently.

Table (2) List of Youth Unemployment Mitigation Labs carried out by the researcher from September 2015 till March 2019.

a) **Direct Youth Unemployment Proactive Approaches (DP)**

Type of Business	Summary of Socio-Economic Type of Inspiring Projects/Models
1. Education for job creators & capacity building for job seekers (DP)	1-Developing creative thinking programs. 2-Discovering Inspiring Students at the right time during their 12 years in education. (Early inspiration discovery program). 3-Establishing track of the inspired students after graduation (Inspiration Pathways). 4- Delivery of (extra-curricular programs). 5-Establishing early inspiration discovery program. 6-Building Inspiration resources within School and after School. 12-Establishing Future Boundary-less Schools

Type of Business	Summary of Socio-Economic Type of Inspiring Projects/Models
2. High Education that creates new labour market (DP)	1-Build a knowledge economy driven practices, including implementation of Lifelong learning skills programs 2-Improve the academic counselling that enhance the students' graduation time and give proper guidance at the right time. 3-Improve the University capability to attract competitive projects and contracts through re-organising its knowledge expertise and profile. 4-Establish better readiness for students lifelong learning skills as per the type of speciality and disciplines. 5-Enhance students' fitness or competence to meet labour market demand. 6-Ensure students finish the requirements of the curriculum in the planned time: i.e., within four years for Bachelor programmes, and one and half years for Masters programmes. 7-Apply Pull-thinking technique to improve academic advisory services. 8-Apply 'smart registration practices' that enhances the students' choices and eliminate waste in opening extra sessions.
3. Labour Market (DP)	1-Shifting Unemployment through inspiring the stratification of Human Capital data and building models in specific industries as per countries sustainable socio-economy needs 2-Minimising unemployment rate through effective counselling 3-Raising opportunities for employment through sourcing type of job opportunities, especially in less demanding jobs 4-Improving locals' employment and demand in areas of hospitality, engineering and nursing 5-Minimise the gap between locals and expat in the main jobs of market demand by defining areas that the national labour should compete.
4. Improving handcrafts in Villages (DP)	Improving the quality of handcrafts finishing and representation in the villages.

Type of Business	Summary of Socio-Economic Type of Inspiring Projects/Models
5. Village Society – Productive Families & Eco-Tourism Program (DP)	1- Collection of small and large projects that target to create a comprehensive eco-tourism village. 2-All projects related to working from home and the provision of raw materials to making gift products, fashion design are inter-related, and this gives more importance to the project. 3-Target is to gradually make the village reach tourist spot with different hospitality activities especially during holidays and specific seasons
6. Graduating and Unemployed Graduate Students Mindset Management (DP)	1-Understanding Dynamics of Labour Market 2-Setting life purposefulness Mindset 3-Challenging transformation towards self-independence and 'Big Picture' Legacy Model 4- Enhancing Employer engagement with schools, colleges and universities and improve the feedback Students interaction and readiness to challenges of the local economy.
7. Women Entrepreneurship NGO (DP)	1-Analysing the impact of programs on 'woman development', not only 'women-empower', and the 'living standards' that comes with the 'Quality of Life' in the NGO area and scope of delivery. 2-Optimising the inter-disciplinary learning approach. 3-Enhancing the 'learning by doing' practices 4-Measure the differentiation of women on the economy.
8. Organic Farming Tourism (DP)	Select areas of Organic Farming and turn it around eco-tourism to enhance the young formers profit margin and quality of life while supporting family continuity and encouragement of youth into this business.
9. Social Insurance (DP)	1-Creating selective thinking in the way of investment of pension fund that would enhance the productivity of the national economy 2-Inspiring the social responsibility plans to ensure that selective type of lower pension jobs is more prepared for entrepreneurship after retirement.
10. Applied Science Colleges (DP)	1-Inspiring students to enhance their scientific and research contribution towards innovation index by more focused projects 2-Use the power of peer to peer influence to improve non-performing students

The Defiance

Type of Business	Summary of Socio-Economic Type of Inspiring Projects/Models
11. Woman Village NGO (DP)	1-Enhance the Return on Capital Employed for the villagers during the chain of making to delivery and distribution 2-Enhance young girls' involvement in Woman village activities to ensure the sustenance of knowledge transfer.

Source: Buheji, M. (2018) Re-Inventing Our Lives, A Handbook for Socio-Economic "Problem-Solving", Appendix (2) AuthorHouse, UK.

b) Indirect Youth Unemployment Proactive Approaches (IP)

Type of Business	Summary of Socio-Economic Type of Inspiring Projects/Models
12. Radio & TV – Bahrain & Bosnia (IP)	1-Build focused positive psychology waves of initiatives that raise the aspiration of the society and trust of the future of the socio-economy of the country 2-Setting inspiration & youth economy focused strategic programs that integrate all the concerned parties towards action
13. Social Development to mitigate Unemployment Risks (IP)	1-Improving the Quality of Life of the Elderly/ Geriatric Care Homes through exploring social asset of Day-Care Homes, instead of permanent residency homes. 2-Inspiring the capacity of the productive family program to be more self-independent and attractive for more family members to join as full-time employees/ owners. 3-Building stronger family businesses that have higher Return on Capital Employed (ROCE). 4-Enhance the return from Elderly homecare production 5-Enhance the quality of life of the Disabled People and their Production 6- Easing the process of home care 7- Supporting 'Working from Home' Program 8- Revaluating the Capability of Social Allowance Value and Entitlement – in relevance to Quality of Life with priorities. 9- Enhancing the quality and competitiveness of the product of the Retired & the Disabled

Type of Business	Summary of Socio-Economic Type of Inspiring Projects/Models
	10- Improving the Quality of Micro Start Families with a focus on Women and People Vulnerability. 11-Improving Quality of Life of Families in isolated communities and tribes (enhance the productivity factors for women and families working from home), with a target to reduce the impact of poverty through eco-tourism projects.
14. Quality Assurance in Education (IP)	1-Ensuring that all students in under-performing school meet the minimal standard. 2-Ensure that QA system create job creators, not job seekers
15. Woman National Planning (IP)	1-Setup a comprehensive outcome and legacy-driven national plan that changes the way woman are empowered in Bahrain by giving her more accountability to create social cohesion, stability and national competitiveness. 2-Closing the gap and accelerating the transformation towards 'Women Development' instead of 'Women Empowerment' after five years from the National Plan Kick-off. 3-Ensure knowledge sharing between Business Women, Women Entrepreneurs and Women of Productive Families Programs and especially those of the same or relevant business and link it to gamification rating. (i.e. Rating of Entrepreneurs who contribute and share knowledge)
16. Humanitarian Services Agency (NGO's) (IP)	1-Reversing the model of poverty support, by making poverty as a temporary condition that we need to prepare the beneficiaries to beyond this stage. 2-Diverting the type of services to be more for sustained income, instead of non-sustainable support 3-Mapping partnership collaboration services (Academic, youth, NGO's, Government, etc.) -Building Cost and Profit centre
17. Socio-Economic Role of School Dormitory (IP)	1-Showing the benefit and the differentiation of the 'Non-Performing Students' towards the Society and the Socio-Economy. 2-Establishing Students micro start companies 3-Establishing model for dealing non-performing students 4-Showing the self-independence of Religious Studies schools and students (by developing more profit rather than cost centre).

The Defiance

Type of Business	Summary of Socio-Economic Type of Inspiring Projects/Models
18. University (IP)	Ensuring Lifelong Learners Students through the inspiring way of flipped class teaching and ensuring suitable preparedness for coming life challenges.
19. Municipalities and Urban Development (IP)	1-Redesigning the public buildings for schools, hospitals to create more multi-purpose buildings owned by the Government and measured for its rate of occupancy and utilisation. 2-Enhance recycling culture and practices, besides prove its financial benefits for decision makers, without increasing resources. 3-Improve Building maintenance facilities in the early stages of government-owned building designs
20. Tender Board (IP)	1-Diverting more tenders to the benefit of local SMEs and new start-ups. 2-Setting performance standard for the role of the tender board in the cycle of the economy.
21. Inspiration Economy Teaching Program in Higher Education (IP)	1-Implementation of Inspiration Economy Diploma Program 2-Illustration by Doing Multi-disciplinary teaching in classes 3-Illustration of how inspiration economy changes the way Course intended learning outcome and the program intended learning outcome through techniques as changing the enablers (i.e. the way teaching is delivered in flip class approach where students teach, and the teacher facilitates) 4-Establish outcomes that are measured by 'open book exam' and by effective projects that enhance the students persistent in creating positive change in the area studies.
22. Management of NGO's role in creating better Socio-Economies (IP)	1-Creating Discussion Group between the different last three generations that identifies: the respected difference, the gaps and positivity of intergeneration gap. 2-Setting projects for mitigation of the gaps
23. Greenhouse project in eco-tourism villages (IP)	1-The project involves many people from the village and youth to produce semi high-end products relevant to what the greenhouse produce. 2-Branding, Packaging, Labelling and Marketing of the semi high- end products of the eco-village. 3-Reduce Migration of Youth with more employment opportunities for the villager's families.

Type of Business	Summary of Socio-Economic Type of Inspiring Projects/Models
24. 'Education on Wheels' & 'Education at Door Steps' Projects (IP)	1-Target to deliver education to rural and isolated communities. 2-Formal and Informal Education for children in slums areas.
25. Agriculture and Farming (IP)	1-Redesign Bahraini farmers' produce by establishing what is called "National Farmers' Day." 2-Improve the distribution chain of local salad by attracting consumers to purchase local vegetables and fruits, and arranging deals between hospitality suppliers and local farmers. 3-Increase Palm Trees implantation by the government, private and the public. 4-Increase Palm tries protections, care, production and by-product industry develop 5-Improve the level of Gardening Competitions
26. Improve learning capacities to lifelong learning citizens on activities (IP)	1-Show influence of Disruptive Education and Multi-discipline on creating more inspiring students 2-Simulation experiments & hands-on to enhance community innovation around the university campus.

Source: Buheji, M. (2018) Re-Inventing Our Lives, A Handbook for Socio-Economic "Problem-Solving", Appendix (2) AuthorHouse, UK.

c) Direct Youth Unemployment Reactive Approaches (DR)

Type of Business	Summary of Socio-Economic Type of Inspiring Projects/Models
27. Psychiatric Services that help mitigation of un-employment Risks (DR)	1-Inspiration of capacity to manage the anxiety to avoid reaching the level of chronic anxiety 2-Reduce the need to treat anxiety with medicines. 3-Reduce suicide ratio due to early treatment of main causalities among youth. 4-Reduce the patients' sick leave due to self-assessments of psycho-sematic symptoms

Type of Business	Summary of Socio-Economic Type of Inspiring Projects/Models
28. Commercial Sector (DR)	1-Enhancement of CR registration through inspiring the reality of 'one stop shop'. 2- Improving the contribution of Microstate and Small Enterprises towards more profitability and enhancing its actual contribution to Labour Market. 3-Improving the speed and availability of fine stones and pearls test certificates 4-Improving the cash flow status of Family Enterprises and reducing bad debts 5-Improving the smooth transition of businesses from 2nd to 3rd generations. 6-Building Independent Business Models 7-Ensuring 2nd generation appreciates the importance of family business governance 8-Raising the capacity, the differentiation of the 2nd generation 9-Setting the smooth transition mechanisms within the families generations.
29. Pension Fund (DR)	Inspiring investment towards enhancement Local Market Stability
30. Labour Fund (DR)	1-Ensuring that all funded projects had made a success story through the domino's effect of Labour Funds. 2-Ensure measurement of success stories in relevance to Labour fund projects 3-Ensuring the developing capacity in the survival of start-ups of more than three years on average and development of safe exits to youth projects. 4-Minimise enterprises' dependency on government aid funds. 5-Divert more mentorship on 'Necessity Entrepreneurship' and improve the solutions they bring to the community.
31. Migrants & Migration Risks Mitigations (DR)	1-Program for healing migrants' psychology and mental healthiness to create from them contributing citizens in the hosting country. 2-Help establishing special Entrepreneurship Companies (using collaborative & knowledge economy techniques) for Migrants youth that accelerate their preparedness for inclusion in the new labour market.

Type of Business	Summary of Socio-Economic Type of Inspiring Projects/Models
	3-Create success stories of sharing economy based models of migrants who came back to re-settle and influence their socio-economy. 4-Enhance migrants' productive families' capability integration in the country of the host.
32. Barbarian farmers Village (DR)	1-Improving the quality of life of families in the Amazigh Villages through eco-tourism and small family businesses that support such cluster 2-Build youth independence program that counters poverty through raising the capacity of the farmers for competitive packaging and distribution. 3-Build youth trust in the village system as a source of income
33. Students Socio-psychology Awareness and counselling programs (DR)	1-Sponsoring project on counselling the students' social workers and councillors 2-Simplify tools for measuring students' safety or positive psychology or stress release 3- Not our goal to do students awareness campaign for universities, but do projects make a university or school bullying, harassment, etc. 4-Tackle issues of students' depression and see its influence on society.
34. Ministry of Labour (DR)	1Re-Engineering Counselling Services to start from High School and be Flexible towards Job Creators than just Job Seekers. 2-Ensuring alternative plans for graduating specialities with constraint opportunities 3-Starting Companies for Unique Jobs as Nursing, Social Workers, Hospitality Services. 4-Nationalising Jobs that represent the country heritage and support tourism 5-Exploring the possibility of creating Human Capital Bank that would transform 30% of the Job Seeker towards job creation; over a planned career path. 6-Closing the Gender Gap in Unemployment, by re-inventing new productivity jobs for Graduating Women.

Source: Buheji, M. (2018) Re-Inventing Our Lives, A Handbook for Socio-Economic "Problem-Solving", Appendix (2) AuthorHouse, UK.

d) Indirect Youth Unemployment Reactive Approaches (IR)

Type of Business	Summary of Socio-Economic Type of Inspiring Projects/Models
35. Bringing Low Privileged Community Children to Formal-Education by focusing on Sports (IR)	1-Integrating youth with both formal sport and traditional games 2-Evaluate possibility for the continuation of formal and informal education 3-Use peer to peer education
36. Housing Services (IR)	1-Reduce the gap between citizens' demands and their quality of life needs 2-Improving the choices and variety of options in non-villa packages (i.e. flats) 3-Reduce the negative social inequality and improve social coexistence through post-housing services
37. Societal Change Programs (IR)	1-Mitigation of Migration amongst Youth 2-Optimise the Youth Quality Life through Students Pull thinking targeted programs 3-Building a poverty blockage and prevention program 4-Addressing the Gambling (pitting) behaviour amongst youth and building prevention scheme through schools' model 5-Building Youth Entrepreneurship & Innovation programs 6-Enhancing Youth contribution in voluntary work through rectifying and supporting a change in Sports club towards enhancing youth decision making. 7-Bridging the gap between academic Social Work and Social Studies Schools and the realised community problems. (Building Life Long Learning Programs that shape the Community) 8-Improving disserted women shelters returns. 9-Improving children without known parents' programs 10-Enhancing Red-Cross Programs Impact in the positive psychology of the community 11-Improving Pre-School influence programs on Children of Homeless and Beggars' families.

Type of Business	Summary of Socio-Economic Type of Inspiring Projects/Models
38. Camel Wool Carpet Factory to be in Villages (IR)	1- Reverse-Design for Camel Wool Factory- Production from the Factory to Production to the Factory 2Re-Distribute Manual Wool Carpet Machines from Factory focused on Villages & Production Families Focused. 3- Re-establish Organic Handmade Carpet Marketing Program
39. Improve the Quality of Life of 'Waste Pickers' (IR)	1-Improve Quality of Life of 'Waste Pickers' Families through differentiating their productivity from Municipalities coming to Waste Management 2-Segregating waste bins implantation in universities, schools & hotels, residential societies 3-Processing of the collected waste into high-end products (i.e. Metals, glass, papers, and organic wastes) processed to high-end products. 4-Improve the Nursery project and ensure the proper distribution channel of Nursery plants

Source: Buheji, M. (2018) Re-Inventing Our Lives, A Handbook for Socio-Economic "Problem-Solving", Appendix (2) AuthorHouse, UK.

Discussion

Causes of Unemployment – Synthesis from Literature

The reviewed literature shows that prime causes of unemployment cannot be list under one category. Although youth do not have much difficulty about occupational immobility, they are today under a consistent challenge to learn new skills and adapt with the high speed of new industrial developments along with the change in technology and geographical immobility.

The other cause of youth unemployment is frictional unemployment which is taken by the individuals while they change their job. The literature also shows that the challenge comes from the type of approaches followed for filling the gap of youth unemployment. i.e. Youth might have seasonal unemployment which takes place due to seasonal change in the job nature as in tourism, fruit picking and hospitality. Hence, this does not solve the problem effectively.

Casual youth employment is a type of employment that comes in, for employees who work on a day to day basis or on short term contracts. Most of the places where casual employment exists for young people are usually based on hard labour as dockyards, market places and rarely film or tech industry.

Effects of Youth Unemployment

The literature shows excellent influence of youth unemployment on the economy and the socio-economy. This is mainly because youth effects nations in their capacity for collecting tax revenues, increasing the supply cost and enhancing welfare cost. With youth being available on the job, we can lower wages, ensure the control of prices on goods and services improve the training quality vs cost, improve the living standards, increase the investors' confidence and minimise knowledge or skills drain.

The issue of youth unemployment does not only affect the SDG achievement, but goes further as shown from literature to affect the country's economic development, especially they are a human capital that makes one-third of the working-age population of all the emerging and developing economies. Since youth in these economies are mostly NEET, i.e. more than 20% of them are neither employed, nor in school or training, this would raise the rate of youth age in entering the market by at least three %t.

Effect of Current Youth Unemployment Policies

The reviewed literature draws on both analyses of different literature that came from both macroeconomics and microeconomic policies. Despite the diverse policies that address this issue, challenges in the youth labour market persist.

There are three major types of public policy: regulatory policy, distributive policy, and redistributive policy. Each type has a special purpose when it comes to youth unemployment. A major goal of all these policies is to maintain order and prohibit behaviours that endanger society. The policies as shown from the literature review either try to accomplish the goal of guiding organisations towards better youth employment or engaging organisations and youth into actions that would positively affect the socio-economic and socio-political order.

Other distributive policies target to enhance the economic activities and businesses that would trigger more youth employment and create a more suitable market for them while redistributive policies would focus on promoting the equality that ensures societal wealth from youth employment and capitalises on the benefits that come from such programs.

In general, once from the synthesis of the reviewed literature, one could say there is no clear evidence for approaches that are made to selecting the right policies based on experimentation or labs. With the high speed of advancement in the technology and socio-economic instability, policies seem not capable of matching the needed gap closure, especially with the slow development of the capacity of the education that meets the market demands. Therefore, testing the approaches through the effectiveness of economic policies may help the young better cope with such market disruptions.

Approaches to Inspiration Labs vs Current Approaches

The inspiration labs followed different approaches to mitigate youth unemployment as a socio-economic issue. The inspiration labs had the following two main approaches:

Proactive Approaches

These approaches address the distributive (the economic development) and redistributive (economic equality) policies; as in the education for job creators and capacity building for job seekers. The proactiveness of these approaches can be either mostly direct proactive, or indirect proactive approaches.

The other proactive approaches are working on inspiring students to enhance their scientific and research contribution towards innovation index by more focused projects. The approach target to prepare youth to take more jobs relevant to scientific and research-based jobs.

One of the focused approaches that could be retrieved from the inspiration labs case study is the selective investment towards enhancing youth role in the local market and setting life purposefulness mindset that suite this initiative. The other unique proactive approach focuses on enhancing the youth employers' engagement with schools, colleges and universities and improve the youth interaction and readiness to the challenges of the local economy. All the proactive approaches work to manage the challenges towards the transformation of self-independence and the 'big picture' legacy model.

Reactive Approaches

The reactive approaches work to mitigate the risks of youth unemployment and help to close the gaps of any significant defect relevant to youth employment or employability efforts and preparations. The approaches here either direct reactive or indirect reactive approaches. For example, the provision of youth-focused psychiatric services that help to eliminate the negative impact of youth unemployment is one of the proactive and still reactive approaches. Same thing when ensuring that all students in under-performing school meet the minimal standard.

Part of the reactive approaches is also ensuring that all youth funded projects have made a success story and properly shared amongst youth in the labour market. In continuation of this establishing special entrepreneurship companies (using collaborative and knowledge economy techniques) for youth, migrants accelerate their preparedness for inclusion in their new labour market and eliminate their immersion in the cycle of poverty.

The strong approaches of the inspiration labs as per Table (2) is the efforts on shifting unemployment through inspiring the stratification of human capital data and building models in specific industries, as per countries sustainable socio-economy needs. These approaches also found to optimise the youth quality life through selectively targeted programs.

Conclusion

To solve the unemployment problem, we need a holistic approach that ensures the development of policies but based on experiential learning and industrial friendly approaches that accept the facts and manage to mitigate the realised risks by actual problem-solving labs and models. Such an approach could speed up the achievement of the UN-SDG regarding youth empowerment and solve the huge gap in relevance to youth unemployment. The chapter shows there are many direct and indirect proactive and reactive approaches to the unemployment of youth that reached a source status and percentages in even developed countries. These approaches can go beyond waiting for decision makers and can start from social, or socio-economic driven business models.

The inspiration labs cases listed in the table (2) show that we humans today should and could bring in more creativity to the issue of youth unemployment, through proactive and reactive approaches that could change our mindset in dealing with such complex socio-economic problem. The case study presents an opportunity for many countries and international organisations working with youth, or on the issue of unemployment, youth migration, or even youth quality of life. It is a list of approaches that might help many communities, directly or indirectly, from different perspectives on how to be both proactive and reactive regarding the issue of youth unemployment and specifically for those youth in NEET.

Despite, the limitations of this study which was carried only in a longitudinal period of 3.5 years and in specific countries, the variety of approaches present many rich possibilities that could be generalised to face the coming economic downturn in both developed and developing countries. The labs presented certainly present a potential shake-up of the classical policies followed and the solution proposed in dealing with such alarming problem that hinders the current and coming generation contribution to the global development, taking that we are living in a thriving and yet turbulent knowledge and innovation-based economy. The holistic approach explored in this chapter shows a new disruptive way of solving such communities' challenges, and it is undoubtedly would open more desires for more future research.

References

Ahn, J; An, Z; Bluedorn, J; Ciminelli, G; Kóczán, Z; Malacrino, D; Muhaj, D and Neidlinger, P (2019) Improving Youth Labour Market Outcomes in Emerging Market and Developing Economies, IMF Staff Discussion Note, Jan. https://www.imf.org/~/media/Files/Publications/SDN/2019/SDN1902.ashx

Amadeo, K (2018) The best way to solve high unemployment according to research, https://www.thebalance.com/unemployment-solutions-3306211.

Anonymous (2108) Unemployment - Policies to Reduce Unemployment
https://www.tutor2u.net/economics/reference/unemployment-policies-to-reduce-unemployment

Buheji, M. (2018a) Book Review- Empowering Young People in Disempowering Times Fighting Inequality through Capability Oriented Policy. Advances in Social Sciences Research Journal, 5(5) 290-291.

Buheji, M. (2018b) Book Review – 'Influence of Modern Welfare State on Socio-Economic Development', International Journal of Youth Economy 2(2),165-167.

Buheji, M. (2018c) Foreword – 'Youth Role in Transforming Change towards a better World', International Journal of Youth Economy 2(2), I-II.

Buheji, M (2018d) Handbook of Youth Economy, AuthorHouse, UK.

Buheji, M. (2018e) Re-Inventing Our Lives, A Handbook for Socio-Economic "Problem-Solving", AuthorHouse, UK.

Buheji, M (2017a) In Search of the Inspired Student—Measuring of Youth Inspiration in High School—A Youth Economy-Paper American Journal of Industrial and Business Management, 7, pp. 785-797,

Buheji, M (2017b) Investigating the Importance of 'Youth Economy', International Journal of Current Advanced Research, Volume 6; Issue 3; March; pp. 2405-2410.

Buheji, M (2017c) Forward- Youth Economy and Utilisation of Lost Opportunities, International Journal of Youth Economy, 1(2): 1-2.

Economic Discussion (2019) Suggestions to Solve Unemployment Problem.
http://www.economicsdiscussion.net/articles/suggestions-to-solve-unemployment-problem/2287

Eshelman, K (2015) Three Ways to Solve Youth Unemployment, Blog Economics, Values and Capitalism.

http://www.valuesandcapitalism.com/three-ways-solve-youth-unemployment/

European Union (2019) SALTO-YOUTH is a network of 6 Resource Centres working on European priority areas within the youth field.
https://www.salto-youth.net/mysalto/login/?pfad=%2Fmysalto%2F

Hadjivassiliou, K; Kirchner, L and Speckesser, S (2015) Key Indicators and Drivers of Youth Unemployment, Institute for Employment Studies (IES), WP3 - Policy Performance and Evaluation Methodologies, Version - 2.0, May.

Johansson, E and Handelshögskolan, S (2015) Who Makes the Transition from Unemployment to Self-Employment? Institutionen för nationalekonomi, FINLAND

KIM, V (2019) In a tough market, young South Koreans vie for the security of government jobs, Los Angeles Times, Feb 6.
https://www.latimes.com/world/asia/la-fg-south-korea-jobs-20190206-story.html

Lagard, C and Bludorn, J (2019) Unlimited opportunities: Creating more jobs for young people in the emerging market and developing economies, World Economic Forum, Feb 6.

Reddy, C (2017) How to Solve Unemployment in a Country
https://content.wisestep.com/solve-unemployment-country-best-tips/

WEF (2018) Youth Unemployment, World Economic Forum.
http://reports.weforum.org/global-risks-2018/youth-unemployment/

WEF (2019) Unlimited Opportunities- Creating more Jobs for Young People in Emerging Market and Developing Economies.
https://www.weforum.org/agenda/2019/02/unlimited-opportunities-creating-more-jobs-for-young-people-in-emerging-market-and-developing-economies-265ff21ae8/

Yahia, A (2018) Estimation of Okun Coefficient for Algeria, International Journal of Youth Economy 2 (1), pp. 1-16.

CONCLUSION

Although a lot has been published about problem solving, this edited book carries new selection of papers that address very important scarce area in the context of socio-economic issues and challenges. The case studies present the defiant spirit that comes along with inspiration labs that target to create breakthrough solutions. These breakthroughs come as a result of problems been seen as sources for discovering more opportunities which bring along better social and economic results and outcomes.

The chapters show that there are minimum success factors that can be used when shaping socio-economic outcomes. The utilisation and operationalisation of complex problem-solving techniques, as the differential diagnosis, help to discover challenging hidden opportunities and the blind spots in chronic problems. The papers, represented by chapters in this book, show how problem-solving is not a commodity, but it is a must for survival and effective future foresight. The competitive economic differentiation and the significant gap closure shed light on in a new area acclaimed by this book that is the economics of problem-solving.

The implementation of inspiration labs shows how to create an 'influencing without power' through creating change in the attitudes towards stages of synergy. The socio-economic value of solving a chronic problem, as the shortage of hospital emergency beds in the country, shows the differentiation that outcome-driven solutions bring.

The capacity for solving socio-economic problems is tested through different approaches, which opens up new paths for the knowledge community. Finally, it is worth to note that the defiant model solutions in this book focus on how to mitigate complex socio-economic issues, especially the ones that are addressed by latest UN-SDG's. We hope this work would open new ideas and more contribution towards future socio-economic challenges, while building also spirit of defiance in the mindset of every problem solver.

MAIN REFERENCES

Ahmed, D and Buheji, M (2018) Reflexivity in Applying "Inspiration Economy" Research: Changing the Game to Make the Research Groups "Researchers", International Journal of Qualitative Methods, Volume 17: 1–8, SAGE Publications.

Buheji, M (2019) Designing a Curious Life, AuthorHouse, UK

Buheji, M (2019) Understanding the Economics of Problem-Solving. A Longitudinal Review of the Economic Influence of Inspiration Labs- Three Years Journey on Socio-Economic Solutions. American Journal of Economics 2019, 9(2): 79-85.

Buheji, M (2019) Influence of visualised reflection on 'solving socio-economic problems' – a case from youth economy forums, Int. J. Innovation and Learning, 25 (1), pp. 1-16.

Buheji, M (2019) Shaping the Anatomy of Socio-Economic Community Problems towards Effective Solutions, Issues in Social Science, Vol. 7, No. 1, pp. 1-11.

Buheji, M (2019) 'The Trust Project' Building better accessibility to Healthcare Services through Behavioural Economics and Inspiration Labs, International Journal of Economics, Commerce and Management, United Kingdom, Vol. VII, Issue 2, February.

Buheji, M. (2018) Re-Inventing Our Lives, A Handbook for Socio-Economic "Problem-Solving", AuthorHouse, UK.

Buheji, M. (2018) Recognising Lives around Socio-Economies? – Foreword, International Journal of Inspiration & Resilience Economy 2018, 2(2): 0-0

Buheji, M and Ahmed, D (2017) Breaking the Shield- Introduction to Inspiration Engineering: Philosophy, Practices and Success Stories, Archway Publishing, FROM SIMON & SCHUSTER, USA.

Buheji, M (2017) Understanding Problem-Solving in Inspiration Labs, American Journal of Industrial and Business Management, 7, pp. 771-784,

Buheji, M and Ahmed, D (2016) Application of Differential Diagnosis in Inspiration Economy Labs – A Literature Review, International Journal of Economic Research, 13(8), 2016: 3681-3687.

Chang, E; D'Zurilla, T and Sanna, L (2004) Social Problem Solving: Theory, Research, and Training.

Szimai, A (2014) Socio-Economic Development, Cambridge University Press, 2nd Edition.

BRIEF ABOUT EDITORS

Dr Mohamed Buheji is the founders of the International Institute of Inspirational Economy and considered a leading expert in the areas of **Excellence, Knowledge, Innovation, Inspiration, Change Management and enhancement of Competitiveness** for over 25 years. He is retired professor from University of Bahrain. Besides being **a Future Foresighter. He** is also the **Founder of the International Journal of Inspiration & Resilience Economy and International Journal of Youth Economy.** He has published since 2008 more than 70 peer-reviewed journal and conference papers and 20 books in the subject of the **power of thinking, lifelong learning, quality of life, inspiration, resilience, youth, curiosity and competitiveness**. Also he has **Eight books in English about Knowledge Economy, Inspiration Economy, Inspiring Government, Inspiration Engineering, Re-Inventing Our Life, Exploring Inspiration Economy, Resilience Economy, Youth Economy and Designing Curious Life.** He is passionate about transferring his + 500 consultancy projects experience for more than 300 organisations from all over the world, to both education and research. In addition, he serves in the editorial board of 5 internationally peer reviewed journals. He is member of many scientific communities, journals, academic review

boards. Lately, he is winner of many awards including the latest **CEEMAN best researcher award for 2017**, besides being a **Fellow of World Academy of Productivity Science.**
Address: International Institute of Inspirational Economy, [e-mail: buhejim@gmail.com,]

Dr Dunya Ahmed Abdulla Ahmed is an **assistant professor** and lecturer in the Department of Social Sciences at the University of Bahrain & **Strategic Planning & Development Adviser** in Supreme Council for Women. In addition, she is **Scientific Committee Chairperson in Institute of Inspiration Economy, EU & MENA.** She completed her PhD at the University of Warwick, to be the first and only person hold a PhD in social work in Bahrain, specialized and concentrates mainly on gender equity and the rights of people with disabilities. She is **co-founder of Inspiration Economy concept, Journals, projects & institutions around the world.** She is also Editorial Board of several international scientific journals. In addition of being an active member of several NGOs & **president of Inspiration Economy Society** in Bahrain. She has also contributed to the preparation and implementation of a number of national strategies, and preparation and discussion of international reports.
Address: Department of Social Sciences, College of Art, University of Bahrain, P.O. Box 32038, Kingdom of Bahrain and Inspiration Economy Society, Kingdom of Bahrain. [e-mail: dr.dunya@hotmail.com]